Investigating
Morals and Values
in Today's Society

by
Paul D. Garnett

illustrated by Paul Manktelow

Cover by Paul Manktelow

Copyright © Good Apple, Inc., 1988

ISBN No. 0-86653-443-1

Printing No. 15 14 13

Good Apple
A Division of Frank Schaffer Publications, Inc.
23740 Hawthorne Boulevard
Torrance, CA 90505-5927

Investigating
MORALS and VALUES
in Today's Society

FOREWORD

Some years ago I put together some considerations for practicing teachers in my *Teacher's Guide to Moral Education* (Chapman, London, 1973). Even then it was apparent that one of the teacher's chief needs was for a practical book, manual or set of materials which reflected the students' interests well enough to arouse their motivation. This need is admirably met by Paul Garnett's book, which most will certainly find of great practical value in engaging students with the problems and excitements of morality.

John Wilson

University of Oxford

TABLE OF CONTENTS

SECTION I: BUILDING THE SELF-IMAGE

SECTION II: THE DYNAMICS OF WORKING IN A GROUP

SECTION III: LEADERSHIP

Being a moral person is not an easy hat for most of us to wear, but it can be easier and more natural after one has mastered the initial skills, just as swimming or riding a bicycle becomes natural after you have once learned how. Unfortunately, failure in morality is often not as obvious as drowning or falling off a bicycle, nor is the moral course to follow as clear as a road map although there always seems to be lots of advice along the way. So much ink has been spilled on the definition of what is good and bad that we should be surprised that the good friar Bacon did not write: " 'What is morality?' said truthful Pilate."

To this pressing problem, the teacher needs to bring some real-life tools to work with if the classroom is to be a positive moral environment beyond being just a think tank. May I propose the following "toolbox" for the teacher to shape and smooth the rough edges of growing young people?

One of the most important aspects of teaching is to develop within the learner a basic transferable skill. Animated, interesting discussions concerning moral dilemmas are stimulating, but often in the end, there is little applicable for the young person to transfer to the perplexing ensemble of events which we call life.

Long philosophical discussions do not resolve moral conflicts; instead, they often leave a residue of confusion. In most moral questions, it is best to emphasize the moral principles and how they may apply. The moral principles should act much like a pair of spectacles, allowing the student to see things more clearly without the tint of cultural bias or environmental distortion. In time, with the application of what is clear, the boundaries of clarity will ever widen, shrinking more and more what is doubtful.

The teacher should avoid moving a moral problem to its extreme position, attempting to demonstrate that some course of action is impossible or unworkable. This approach is often called "reductio ad absurdum" and may produce elegant results in logic, but in moral education it demonstrates the moral educator's lack of confidence to really come to grips with the hard kernel of the problem. It is easy to flee to some secure, absolute position which relieves the moral practitioner of all thoughtful consideration of the factors and outcomes of the case. This produces more than an inclination to use existing prejudices; it is the creation within your students of instant prejudices, which may be far worse than the problem under consideration.

Editor's Note: It is advisable that the teacher use discretion in selecting the material to be used in a given classroom situation. The overall composite of the class should be considered when dealing with some of the more sensitive issues covered. While some of the material in this book may be controversial, it is impossible to deal with the subject of morality without touching upon sensitive issues.

In real life most moral situations are vague, interrelated and subjectively defined; further, they must be evaluated with all the pertinent factors shifting. If a jury could clearly see whether a defendant was innocent or guilty, there would be no need for juries; the information could be quickly fed into a computer and the verdict would instantly appear on the "read out."

Unfortunately, our society in general, and the young person in particular, has no magic computer to "print out" solutions to moral problems. He must play the game as the parameters shift even worse; in many cases he may find himself in a fast moving, confusing conflict in which the rules are unknown to him. Certainly, the coach (teacher) may help by clearly delineating some basic principles to play by. This perhaps, may permit the student to at least play in the twilight instead of the dark. What then are the basic moral principles? To begin with, in order for us to accept them as principles, they must have the same attributes as the general principles of medicine (legal,

etc.) or any body of thought. These attributes are at least threefold: (1) Moral principles must be universal. They must act upon all cultures in all periods of history, from antiquity to the present; from the mud huts of Africa, to the cloisters of the most sophisticated university. (2) Moral principles must also be independent of personal knowledge of them. Ignorance of these

principles does not make one immune from the consequences. (3) Moral principles must predict the future of a given set of circumstances. Given a set of conditions, moral principles must predict the result or outcome of these factors, just as the law of gravity will predict the result if you step off a roof. The clearer the input, the more definite the predicted outcome.

In view of these attributes, may we suggest the following three moral principles:

I. *Do Unto Others as You Would Have Them Do Unto You.*

(Confucius, 513 B.C.)

II. *The End Does Not Justify the Means.*

(Immanuel Kant, The Critique of Judgement, Part II*)

III. *You Reap What You Sow.*

(The Talmud [Proverbs] Judeo-Christian Tradition)

Corollary a: You reap MORE than you sow.
Corollary b: There is a latent period between sowing and reaping.
Corollary c: The harvest is ALWAYS the same in kind as the seed that is planted.
*"Always act towards the other as an end, not as a means.
Always choose only what you would be willing to have
everyone choose in your situation."

It is not difficult to find counterparts to each of these principles of interpersonal behavior in the realm of nature. Principle I has its counterpart in the electronics of the FeedBack Loop (inanimate) and the physiological principle of homeostasis (animate). In both of these, the external conditions are constantly changing and are being fed back into the system in order for it to adjust accordingly. In the field of interpersonal relationships this same process occurs from day to day as we interact with those around us. The individual finds the world speaks to him in the same tone as he addresses those around him.

The counterpart of Principle II we find in the molecular chemistry of crystalography (inanimate) and in ontogeny of the embryo (animate). Since Principle II is a process, we find crystalography and ontogeny are also very definite processes. When the process is altered (steps omitted), the end result is always different and never as elegant as when all the steps are adhered to. In the moral realm, we cannot omit or use a mischievous method to achieve what we consider to be a virtuous end without changing the desired final situation itself.

Principle III we find in physics as the Law of Cause and Effect. On an interpersonal basis, one can appreciate (or suffer) from the effect of a single moral act or the accumulated effect of a series of moral acts resulting in a single final decisive result.

Like natural laws, these principles must be in harmony with each other but on differential levels of response. Thus we see the first principle describes the ongoing dynamics of moral relationships; the second principle describes a process or a particular sequence of a series of acts with a definite goal; and the third principle describes a single act or the single result from a series of acts, forming a continuum of behavior spanning all aspects of personal and interpersonal relationships.

This text has been organized to give cognitive evaluation a threefold approach which can be shown in the following diagram:

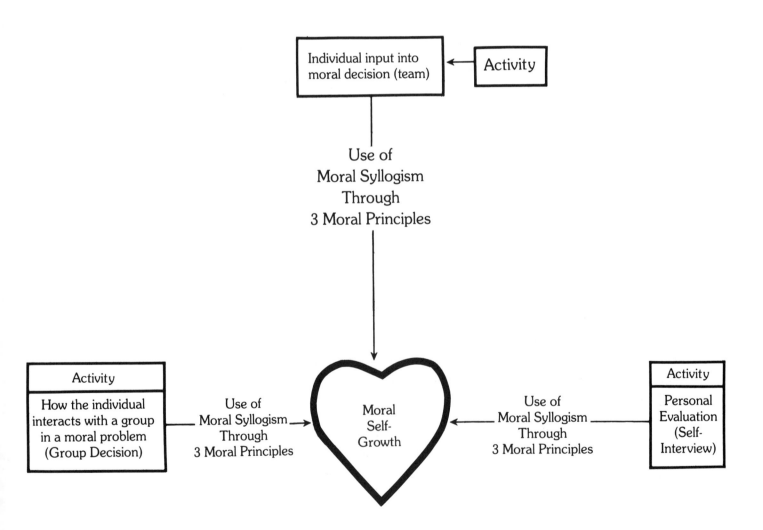

Let us consider how each of these strategies is implemented.

I. The Questionnaire (individual moral decisions)
    The "Self-Interview" on a Moral Topic

Factors:
a. The questions of the self-interview are highly structured in order to give a high degree of reliability (repeatability), permitting easy scoring and self-evaluation.
b. The questionnaire must appear interesting and amusing in order to mask the hidden probe into moral attitudes; otherwise, the results will produce artificial answers which simply match current social mores, failing to give the student a realistic insight into this actual moral stance.
c. Evaluation of the self-interview should center on the proposition: Does the "real you," as revealed by your score, need reassessment in view of the moral syllogism?

II. The Moral Problem (individual input into a group decision on a moral problem)

Factors:
Each student after considering the moral problem, should complete a work sheet which should contain at least five sections as follows:
a. Section I should be an analysis and clarification of the issue. Each of the various factors and conclusions concerning the issue should be subjected to verification of the facts rather than based on casual opinion.
b. Section II should be an application of the conclusions arrived at in Section I. Here the teacher should look for consistency between analysis and conclusions.

c. Section III would be a reminder that before conclusions are arrived at, the decision maker should check to make sure the sources of information are reliable, avoiding those which have a vested interest of bias toward a particular conclusion.

d. Section IV. Having done his "homework," the student is now ready to make his individual decision based on the moral syllogism.

e. Section V. In the final section, the student must now predict the consequences of his decision and its possible outcome in view of the moral syllogism.

III.   The Morals of a Group (how the individual interacts with the group in a moral problem)

Factors:

a. Moral decisions almost always involve others, usually a group. The influence is two-way: you-they and they-you. Which predominates? Should the individual's moral syllogism be put aside for the sake of group harmony? Here the teacher may have the students consider Bishop Shean's statement: "Wrong is wrong if everyone is wrong, and right is right if no one is right."

b. Discussion should center on the question: How does one exert moral leadership? One approach is to look at historical examples, perhaps comparing athletic heroes with social leaders, showing the essential factors of control and know-how. (Wilburforce and Lincoln; Borge and Bruce Jenner)

c. The evaluation should be centered on the question: Was the individual's moral syllogism altered to match the group or vice versa?

From the examples presented here, not only may the teacher develop an overt curriculum of moral education, but with the fun activities there also emerges a "hidden curriculum," both of which may be unified in the discussion sections using the moral syllogism for the child to rectify his present moral stance.

Properly used, the ideas in this text may provide a break for the student and a breakthrough for the administrator looking for a new approach to moral education. To the teacher it may provide some answers to the child's important question: "What do I do now?"

Too many teachers, overwhelmed by the problems of moral education, have said, "I resign." Perhaps now with a few workable moral principles, they will be encouraged to say, "I re-sign."

**Whitewashing the pump
Doesn't make it give pure water.
That must come from down inside the well.**

WE ALL MAKE WAVES

Have you ever stood at a bridge and dropped a rock or a pebble into the water down below? Remember what happened? When the pebble struck the water, waves went out in all directions until finally they reached the bank on each side.

That's something of the same thing which happens every day by things that we say and things that we do. They make little ripples in the lives of the people that go on and on, sometimes for years and years long after they're said or long after they're done. These little ripples affect everybody around us.

Let's say this morning you happen to see somebody who looks depressed and unhappy, and you flash a nice big smile. He feels much better right away. Instead of being unpleasant with the next person he meets, he smiles, and that person feels good also. Let's say that

the person feels so good, he decides he will do some kind, gracious act to someone else, helping him out in some little way. So the smile that you started with has made ripples among many, many people—more than you can imagine.

Of course, the reverse is true. If you scowl at someone or snap at him in the morning because you don't feel well or you're feeling grouchy, then perhaps he will be unkind to the next person he meets. Who knows all of the unpleasant feelings that you may spread among people before the day is over just because of some thoughtless, unkind little ripple that you began when the day started.

One day a young person was chatting with his grandfather and he said to him, "What makes you so happy all the time, Grandpa? In fact, I don't even know anybody that seems happier and more contented than you are."

The grandpa smiled as he thought for a moment; then he said, "You know, when I was young, I was tempted to do all the bad things. But my dad came to me and he said, 'Jerry, a man can never be happy when he gets old if he's shut up inside with a lot of memories of all the things that he did that he wished that he hadn't done. It takes a lot of right living to make life really worthwhile.' I always remembered what my dad told me, and I found out that as I went through life he was right.

"The best way to be happy is to do good to other people. The best way to get from people is to give to them in the first place. That advice which my daddy told me a long, long time ago has made many, many ripples and it's proved to be a real blessing to me and really good advice."

Little things we do and little things we say have far-reaching effects into the lives of others around us. Maybe you think that the little things that you did this morning will be forgotten before the day is over, but that is not true.

Every little act that we do during the day has an effect upon others and their attitudes go on to affect other people around them.

There is an old saying which says, "Don't make waves." Maybe we should change that into, "Don't hesitate to make ripples, ripples of smiles and kind acts throughout the day."

Linda's Diary

Dear Diary,

Today many different things happened to me. They all began this morning when my alarm radio went off at its usual time. The music was so neat, I thought I would just lie there and listen to it for a while. It was almost twenty minutes later when I finally rolled out of bed. I knew I would be late for my first period class, so I yelled downstairs to my mother to forget breakfast. She was very upset since she had fixed my favorite French rolls.

When I arrived at my first period class, everyone was looking at me, so I just ignored them all and smiled at my boyfriend, Peter.

The teacher was talking about the chapter test for tomorrow, telling the class she was going to spend the period in special review. I knew I should listen because I've just been so busy on the telephone, and with TV I just haven't had time to do the assignments. I decided it would be better for me to spend the time studying for my math midterm which was the next period. Besides, I was sure that Peter would help me tonight anyway.

On my way to the math test the next period, I had a great idea. Why not go to the health room instead of taking the math test? So I did. I arrived back at my math class halfway through the test. When I handed my health room excuse to the teacher, he said that I have to come in after school and make it up on my own time. These darn teachers have no consideration of how important my time is.

At lunch Peter met me in our usual spot. He reminded me that we were going to attend a special meeting for college tuition grants. When he asked me if I had filled out my application yet, I had to tell him about how difficult my parents have been lately and that I was waiting for them to be in a better mood to discuss it with them.

Peter said it was OK, we would go to the meeting anyway. At the meeting, they announced late applications would not be considered. The counselor assured Peter that he probably wouldn't have any trouble getting his tuition grant since his application was on time and well written.

Peter asked me if I thought my folks would be able to send me to college without the tuition grant. I had to tell him that Dad had said definitely, "No." Then Peter said he thought that was too bad because he felt we would have made a great team together in college.

I told him we could still team up tonight to study for our first period class test tomorrow, but he said he already knew the work and he had some other things to do.

Boys are just so unreliable!

Well, it's very late and I must try to get up early and study for my test tomorrow, so good night, diary.

Activity

Tell the class you are going to read from a very secret document—the personal diary of a student. Ask how many have kept a diary at one time.

Caution them to listen carefully as this person tells about what happened to her on a particular day. Make notes about her actions during the day and try to determine what kind of person she is, how old she is, and how she affects the lives of others.

Questions for class discussion: (after reading the diary)
1. Would you like to have Linda as a close friend?

2. What kind of person is she?

3. What was the most important thing that happened during the day she writes about?

4. Is Linda a good person, an average person, or a bad person?

5. If Linda were your friend, what would you say to her?

THE STORY OF JOSEPH

It was not unusual for a family long ago to have many children. Such a large family was that of Jacob, a sheepherder. The eldest son was Reuben; the youngest one was Joseph. Unfortunately, Jacob showed a definite favoritism for Joseph, a lad who was apparently able to foretell the future from dreams.

One day Joseph told his older brothers that he had dreamed that they would bow down to him. This dream and their father's favoritism enraged them against Joseph. Away from view, out on the sheep range one day, they decided to kill him, so they threw him into a deep hole thinking they would go off and leave him to die. Reuben, however, felt sorry for Joseph and called his brothers together, proposing that they make some money off the boy by selling him as a slave to some passing Egyptian merchants.

Upon returning home, they showed Jacob the fine coat of many colors which he had given Joseph as a special present. It was torn and covered with blood. Jacob didn't know that the brothers had ripped it and dipped it in the blood of a dead goat; he was grief stricken with the thought that his favorite son had been destroyed by a wild beast.

The brothers, now rid of Joseph, enjoyed the profits and good life from the flocks of sheep and goats their father had accumulated. They enlarged their efforts to plant grain and developed a very prosperous ranch.

Everything went well until one year the rains failed to come. Fortunately they had enough to get them through to the next year, but that spring and summer were hot and dry also. By the third year, they realized that they were now in a prolonged drought and that unless they did something about it they and all their families would starve to death.

From passing merchants they learned that there was plenty of food down in Egypt, since the king's chief minister had foreseen that a great drought was coming and had stored away great supplies of grain. They all agreed that the best thing to do was to hurry down to Egypt to buy whatever food the Egyptians would sell them.

Upon their arrival they were pleased to be greeted by the king's chief minister himself. He asked them a lot of probing questions about where they were from and about their father and even about Benjamin, the youngest of the family who had been left at home with Jacob.

Suddenly, he ordered them put into prison. "He must think we are spies," said Reuben. But a few days later they were freed and permitted to return home with their sacks filled with grain. When it became time to leave, however, they were told that Simeon would be kept as a hostage until they returned with Benjamin the youngest.

How happy everyone was to see the pack animals loaded with grain enough to last them for months; but when they opened their sacks there was all the money they had paid in the top of each sack. Should they return and give it back? "No," said their father, "perhaps they would be arrested again for stealing."

The hot sun continued to burn down and in a few months the food was all gone and they were forced to return to Egypt. This time they had to take Benjamin along. The king's chief minister released Simeon, they filled their sacks with food and started north again; but this time they were stopped by some of the king's soldiers. "You have stolen my master's great silver cup!" said one of the soldiers. When the sacks were opened it was Benjamin's which held the silver cup. The chief minister told them sternly that he would let them go but that he would keep Benjamin because of the theft as his own personal slave.

"I beg you, Your Excellency," pleaded Judah, "take me instead; it will surely be the death of our father to lose his youngest son."

Suddenly, the king's chief minister began to weep. "I can stand it no longer," he said. "I am your brother Joseph, the lad you sold into slavery so many years ago. I forgive you for the wrong you did me. Please bring our father to this land, and I will see that he and all of you are well cared for."

All the brothers enbraced Joseph and they all joined in a tearful reunion. When the Egyptians heard what had happened, they all marvelled at the mercy and love Joseph showed his brothers.

Activity

To the teacher:

Review chapter one of this text which outlines the three moral principles and discuss them with your class before this discussion section.

Questions for discussion:
1. What is the most important thing that happened in this story?
2. Can you give an example from the story of:
   I. Moral Principle
   II. Moral Principle
   III. Moral Principle
3. What would have happened if Joseph had imprisoned his brother permanently?
4. The brothers wished to get rid of Joseph (the end) by murdering him (the means). Reuben said, "We can accomplish our aim (the end) by another way without committing murder (a different means).

   What would have ultimately happened to the brothers if they had ignored Reuben and insisted that the end DOES justify the means?
5. In what ways did Joseph try to implement all three moral principles?

FOLLICULUS FOLLY

(An ancient English folk legend)

Knights of old not only loved their horses, but also their dogs. This was particularly true of a famous warrior knight named Folliculus and his hunting dog, Boris. As Folliculus rode through the forest, Boris's long, lean figure raced ahead of him, chasing game and barking to warn his master of the presence of strangers. Dog and master became very close.

Then one day, a son was born to Folliculus, and Boris was ignored as the new father spent hours in the infant's bedroom playing and chatting with his rosy-cheeked little baby. At first Boris was puzzled that his master no longer took him hunting, but the dog soon sensed that the child was someone his master held very dear, so he would sit outside the nursery door knowing his master would eventually come by.

One day Folliculus was called into the nearby town to greet the king. When he and his wife were about to leave, he patted Boris on the head saying, "Be a good dog, Boris, and guard our child well while we are gone." Then he leaned over and kissed the child and set off for the town.

Upon his return, the first thing he did was to hurry immediately to his baby son, opening the door quietly and tiptoeing into the nursery. He was halfway across the room when he suddenly realized something was terribly wrong. The crib was tipped over with the bedclothes scattered about the floor. Here and there were pools of blood among the cradle blankets. Folliculus was filled with thoughts of horror as he surveyed the disarray. There stood Boris panting with blood on his muzzle and clots adhered to his fur.

"How could you do such a thing?" he cried to the dog he had loved so much. Then in a blind surge of rage he drew his sword and ran it through his dog in a single stroke. Boris sank to the floor with pleading eyes toward his master. Just then, Folliculus caught sight of a slight movement under the bedclothes. With the tip of his sword, he flicked the blanket away and there lay his small son unharmed and full of smiles to see his daddy.

Beside the child lay a great snake, dead now, but clearly bearing on his body the many teeth marks of Boris. Obviously the dog had sprung to the defense of the child when the reptile had attacked the crib.

Folliculus sank to his knees, his sword falling to the floor. Tears flooded his eyes as he embraced the body of his faithful dog. "Ah, what have I done? You saved my baby and I repaid you with a sword thrust. If I had only made sure first! If I had only thought before I acted!"

From that day forward, Folliculus made sure he never acted in haste, but always with thoughtful care, knowing that a sudden mistaken act can sometimes never be made right.

Activity

To the teacher:

Prepare three boxes: 1 wrapped with a fancy covering and a bow
1 wrapped in plain brown paper
1 wrapped in dirty newspaper

Into the first box, put something inexpensive (like a paper clip), into the second put a dollar or coin, and into the last put something very valuable (jewelry). Do not permit the class to see the boxes until you show them one by one.

Hold the first box up and ask the children:

(1) Would you like to know what's inside of it? (Shake it to show that it does contain something.)

(2) Do you think it is something worthwhile? (Take a consensus and write on the board: valuable, not valuable, no value.)

Do the same with each box, showing the dirty box last.

Now open boxes to show their contents and compare with consensus.

Questions for discussion:
1. Can you tell what is inside a box by its appearance?

2. Are people like boxes with different wrappings?

3. Is it a good idea to "jump to conclusions" with people or in a given situation? Or is it best to reserve judgement?

4. Have you ever jumped to the wrong conclusion about something? Tell about it.

5. Have you ever been judged unjustly because someone jumped to conclusions?

6. Having drawn a wrong conclusion and wrongly judged a person or situation, can the wrong be rectified?

PERSONAL

During the Middle Ages, in a very small town, there was a religious woman who decided that it was time for her to go to the village priest to confess her sins. One of the sins that she confessed was that of gossiping.

For penance, the priest ordered her to fill a basket full of feathers and put a few in the backyard of each one of the neighbors about whom she had gossiped.

She went out and gathered the feathers carefully putting them into the backyards of each of the people she had gossiped about. Having completed her penance, she went back to tell the priest that she had done what he had asked her to and that now her penance was complete.

"Oh, no," said the priest. "Now you must go back into the backyards of each of the people and gather up all the feathers again."

She immediately protested, "But I cannot do that. By now the wind has scattered them everywhere."

"Exactly," agreed the priest. "And that is what happens when you tell things about other people that should be kept confidential."

Gossip spreads so fast and so quickly that you are unable to go back and gather up what you have said. None of us can call back the words which once we have spoken.

Why do people gossip about others? One reason is to create excitement. People enjoy seeing others emotionally stirred up when they talk about their friends and neighbors. They like to be the center of attention. Being the first one to know and the first one to tell makes them feel very important.

Secondly, people gossip to entertain their friends. In this case, maybe the original information isn't entertaining enough, and so they'll add to it in order to generate more response on the part of the listener. They don't stop with what they've heard; they add to it.

As one woman said to another on the telephone, "I'll not go into all the details with you. In fact, I have already told you more than I have heard myself."

Another reason some people gossip is to injure someone they don't trust, or a group they don't have membership in. Very rarely does a person gossip about a friend or about a select group of which he is a member.

When is it right to tell facts about others, not gossip, but really known, proven facts? If the story is true, isn't it all right to repeat it?

Often there are things which are absolutely true but should not be told to others. Imagine, for a moment, yourself in the place of the person that is being gossiped about. Suppose you had done something foolish that you regretted, something wrong that everyone knows about? Would it not be unkind for people to tell about things that you yourself were sorry that you had done?

Before you repeat gossip about other people, ask yourself whether you would like to have such things said about you, if you had done the same foolish, unwise things. Gossip helps nobody, not even the one who spreads it.

Activity

To the teacher:

If your class is seated in rows, they will already be organized for this version of an old favorite fun game. If they are not seated in rows, line them up in rows of five or more and you are ready to play.

Type or write out one of the following statements for each row. Give the written statement to the first person in each row. He is to turn around and whisper it into the ear of the person sitting behind him and so on back to the last person in the row.

When the last person has heard the message, he comes up front. He states what he has heard; then the first person reads what the original message said. This usually leads to a humorous situation, permitting the teacher to point out how gossip distorts the truth.

Are girls worse gossips than boys? Try this same game with a girls' team and a boys' team to see who is the more accurate. This now turns into a good listening exercise.

List of statements (or make up your own):

1. Nothing is more annoying than to have someone NOT tell you a piece of gossip you said you didn't want to hear.

2. A loose tongue can lead to a few loose teeth.

3. A wise man thinks without talking, but fools reverse the order.

4. As a person grows older and wiser, he talks less and says more.

5. You can borrow money cheaper than you can marry it.

6. Gossip is one thing that has to be bad for it to be good.

7. Some girls are like candy bars, half sweetness, half nuts.

8. The problem with leisure time is to keep other people from spending it for you.

9. Whether a man ends up with a nest egg or a goose egg depends upon the chick he marries.

10. Those who deserve love the least usually need it the most.

For dramatic effect, if you have two students who speak a foreign language in your class, have them come up in front of the class with two English-speaking students. Put the two double language students in the middle and repeat the game.

Activity

Questions for discussion:

1. Is hearsay evidence admitted in a court of law? Why?

2. Is it OK to tell a "little white lie" that helps someone? (Example: "There really IS a Santa Claus.)

3. What is the difference between "political expediency" and lying? Between "good business" and cheating?

4. How would you treat the rumor that everyone is going to get an "A" in this course?

5. Does the public news media publish (broadcast) rumors and hearsay about people?

SLOW PEOPLE NEVER MAKE IT

The big clock in the jeweler's window stopped one morning at 8:20 a.m. Something had gone wrong with it so it didn't run. The young people on their way to school that morning looked at the clock and stopped to play because they thought they had lots of time. Other people who were hurrying to catch the bus to go to work slowed down and began to walk more slowly because they thought they had plenty of time. A doctor on his way to the office stopped to chat to some other businessmen because he thought he had lots of time. Everyone was late simply because the jeweler's clock, which had always been so reliable, suddenly stopped.

Most people say, "What difference do a few minutes make?" The difference is that once the few minutes are gone, they can never be brought back. Those few minutes not only belong to us, but they also belong to others.

If you are ten minutes late getting to school in the morning, you've lost several good things that the teacher had to say about the class and about the school program before the day began. The teacher may have to say those same things all over again just for your benefit, and that will mean a loss of time for everybody who had been there on time.

What about the man who's late on the job? Suppose he gets there just ten minutes late every day for 24 working days in a month. That means he's been 240 minutes late, or 4 hours that he didn't work that he was supposed to. If the man was getting paid, let's say $2.50 an hour, then he has actually cheated his employer out of $10.00 a week. It's just as though he had stolen $10.00 from the cash register because the employer will be paying him for time in which he did nothing.

Being late to social functions is not only bad taste, but it is also impolite. The members of Congress who always arrived late were surprised one day when they responded to a dinner invitation of General George Washington. When they came they discovered President Washington sitting at the table already eating upon their arrival. He responded to them very courteously saying, "Gentlemen, we are too punctual for you. I have a cook who never asks whether the company has come or not, but merely whether the hour has come."

It's very important for any kind of appointment always to be there a few mintues early instead of a few minutes late. This is especially true if you are going to be interviewed for a job and doubly true if you are going to see a doctor because there are others waiting when you are finished to take up his time.

The man who is late for little appointments in life will also be late for the big appointments in life. When it comes time to graduate, when it comes time to get married, or when it comes time to get that promotion on the job, he'll be late for those things and probably won't even realize what he has missed. Promptness pays off by telling people you are careful about time, both theirs and yours.

Activity

To the teacher:

Have your students fold a sheet of paper vertically down the middle. On the LEFT side they should write either yes or no to the following questions. (Urge them to be as honest as possible.)

1. Are you upset if the teacher continues class after the period is over?

2. Does it bother you if your favorite TV program is suddenly rescheduled to some other time or it is cancelled?

3. Do you mind waiting in front of a movie theater for your friend to come and join you?

4. Does it make any difference to you whether the game starts on time?

5. Do you care if a salesperson comes immediately to wait on you when you are shopping?

6. When you have something fixed, do you mind if it is not finished when it was promised?

7. Does having to wait in the doctor's office upset you when you were on time for your appointment?

8. Do you get impatient and angry if you have to wait for a bus which is late?

9. When you call someone on the telephone does it bother you if you have to "hold the line" for a long time?

10. Do you mind if you get your allowance (paycheck) a couple of days after it was due?

Now have your students turn their papers over to the RIGHT side and answer the following questions either yes or no as honestly as they can.

1. Are you occasionally late for class?

2. Do you ever continue to watch TV when you know you are supposed to be someplace else?

3. Have you ever been late meeting a friend who was waiting for you in front of a movie theater?

4. Do you find yourself getting to the game after it has started?

5. Knowing you are probably going to have to wait at the doctor's office, do you sometimes get there late?

6. Do you not know the EXACT time this class begins?

7. Do you have trouble turning in your term papers the day they are due?

8. Are you sometimes a little late to pay someone back the money you owe them?

9. Do you occasionally return library books after the due date?

10. Do you think most people wear wristwatches just because they like the looks of them?

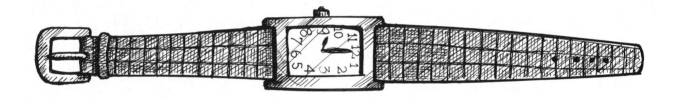

Your students can now open up their answer sheets and score themselves.

A. Any yes answer for the first (left) side is cancelled by any yes answer on the second (right) side, so any two yeses score zero.

B. All no answers score 1 point.

C. Any yes or no on the first (left) side with an opposite response on the second (right) side is scored ½ point.

Ranking:

20 to 15	Very punctual
15 to 10	Above average consideration of others
10 to 7	Average
7 to 5	Below average consideration of others
Less than 5	You are a loser. Better take a serious look at your punctuality.

THE UGLY SIDE OF BEAUTIFUL
(Animal Fable)

The One day all the animals gathered together on the grass in a forest opening just to have a nice chat with one another. It wasn't long until the peacock mounted a tall stump and said, "My friends, listen. I have a question for you. My cousin the guinea hen and I have been having a discussion about who is the handsomest animal of us all. Could you please tell us the answer to this question?" Deep down inside he smiled for he knew they must name him as the most beautiful animal of all.

There was a short silence. Then the hippopotamus raised his great hulk before the group and began to speak with great learned authority.

"My fellow creatures great and small, this is a question to which I have given a great deal of careful thought. In considering the handsomest creature among all of us, we can first exclude the little animals including the birds. They are much too small to be thought of; some may be pretty, but handsome? No, not really. To be considered handsome, an animal must have a great size-commanding appearance with large lines and a big figure that can be seen by all from a distance. I really don't know how to say this, my friends, and I hope you won't think that I have an oversized ego about this, but the only one among us to fit this description is me, the hippopotamus."

All the rest of the animals immediately broke out with laughter, jeers and moans which grew louder and louder until finally, the rhinoceros' deep voice rose above the din.

"Quiet! Quiet, everyone! As strange as it may seem, there really is something in what the hippo has to say. After all, there is something definitely attractive about an animal who demands attention by his size and great bulk, so we really should rule out all the little fellows like birds and butterflies. When you come right down to it, it's really the face that counts and to have a handsome face, one needs something very special . . . like a hair horn such as mine. It's obvious that there is no other animal with such a distinctive feature as mine; surely you must agree if I modestly suggest the rhinoceros as the most beautiful of us all."

Again, all the other animals began to laugh and jeer. The monkey got up and paraded around with his thumb in the middle of his face trying to act like a rhinoceros, an act which got a lot of laughs. Finally, the peacock rose again.

"I really am greatly surprised at all this talk. I expected some sensible answers, but instead all we've heard so far are these big lumbering braggarts making absolutely ridiculous claims. I ask you now, which of us has the most beautiful coloring?" With this, he spread his tail plume, extended for all to admire.

Whistles, yells, jeers followed from all the other animals. A great giant roar of the lion silenced them all.

"We've all heard enough of this. Let us listen to what the owl has to say."

A great silence followed with all eyes turned on the owl. "You animals are as bad as some humans I know, although they often show themselves to be as ruthless and self-centered as some of you. Each one of them thinks he is better because he is taller or shorter, darker or paler, stronger or smarter than someone else. You seem to be the same way. The hippo admires his size, the rhino is proud of his horn and the peacock thinks he's beautiful because of his feathers.

"The truth, my friends, is that there is no such thing as the handsomest creature of us all. Each of us has something special about him, which can be admired, but that doesn't make him better than the rest of us because each of us has our own faults also. The hippo has a quick temper, the rhino has bad eyesight, and the peacock is so vane that ·he started all this controversy. The question is silly and has only one answer; that is: We are all a little beautiful and a little ugly. The best thing is to concentrate on the beautiful in others and minimize the ugly in ourselves."

Activity

To the teacher:

Suggest to your class that it is possible to tell something about a person without ever formally meeting or talking to him, by simply carefully observing his appearance.

Make a ditto, or put the following list on the board:

Effect

1. Hair: long _____ short _____ how kept _____ _____

2. Glasses: (contact lenses?) _____

3. Beard or makeup _____

4. Shirt or blouse _____

5. Slacks or skirt (belt) _____

6. Shoes, sandals _____

7. Wristwatch, jewelry _____

8. School notebook, texts (what is written on them?) _____

9. Purse or wallet (what is in it?) _____

10. Is there any one thing that catches your eye? _____

11. My conclusion about this person is that he wishes to convey the image of _____

Have your class fill out the appearance inventory for you, the teacher, first. Stand up in front of them and respond to any questions they may have. After they have completed the list for you, read several of them (from volunteers) and discuss their conclusions. Usually this can be done with a little humor, and it will relax the group so they will be ready to record their impressions of each other.

Tell them this is a fun game but also very informative for everyone. Have them split up into groups of five and complete their inventory sheets about one another.

For more candid results, these sheets could be anonymous, bearing only the name of the person being observed.

THE TEACHER WHO TAUGHT
ONE OF THE GREATEST LESSONS OF ALL
The Story of Booker T. Washington (1856-1915)

It is hard to imagine how any young person in America could have had a worse start in life than Booker T. Washington. He was born a slave in an open lean-to shack on a southern cotton plantation. His father had deserted his mother, who worked as a cook preparing food for the other slaves working in the fields.

When Booker was old enough, he was given the job of carrying water to the other black plantation workers as they toiled in the hot sun culturing and working the cotton plants. Occasionally, he was given the privilege of going up to the big house to pull the rope operating the cooling fan all evening. There he met the daughters of his white owners and was asked to carry their books to school.

He did this faithfully every day, but he was never permitted to enter the schoolhouse. Instead he would stand outside watching the white children learn to read and write, aching to learn how to open the treasure house of knowledge stored in books. Since there was no school for black slaves, Booker could only watch and wish.

The bloody struggle of the Civil War swept over the plantation, and when Booker was nine years old the slaves were freed. Booker now found himself working twice as hard since his mother remarried and his new stepfather put him to work in a salt mine. All his wages were snapped up by his stepfather, and he had only one shirt which he wore all year long both summer and winter.

Yet, Booker did not give up his quest for knowledge. He begged his mother to get him a book, any book. One day she brought home a spelling book. None of the other Blacks in the salt mine could read in order to help him, so Booker carefully taught himself each of the letters and then sorted out each word, working late into the night after an exhausting day in the mines.

Great news came one day that a teacher was going to set up a school. "Ah," thought Booker, "now I can really learn." But his stepfather would not permit him to attend because he did not want to lose Booker's wages. Finally, after much pleading, Booker was permitted to go if he promised to work from 4 until 9 o'clock in the morning. Imagine yourself working all night before coming to school, and you will have an idea of what it was like for poor Booker.

When he was 16, Booker walked many miles to the next town to attend the academy school. Since the lessons had to be paid for, he persuaded the principal to give him a job as a custodian. On weekends he worked in a local restaurant to buy good clothing. Finally it came time for him to graduate, which was a great distinction and honor. Although he was very young, he immediately was asked to become the teacher back at his own village school.

As Booker taught young black lads, he was reminded of himself years before. He came to the conclusion that only education could free his people from poverty and social degradation which so long had trapped him. He was determined to do something about it, so later when he received an offer to open a black school at Tuskegee, he jumped at it.

On his way to Tuskegee he thought of how he could finally accomplish all he had been dreaming of; but when he arrived there what he found was an old wooden, leaky church building and a rotting cabin. As he swung open the creaking door he discovered the place to be filled with cobwebs with no desks, chairs or books. Worst of all there were no students.

Booker was used to hard work. In a short time he had the place in order and opened the school to its first class of 30 students. Together they built a three-story building on a piece of ground which they had cleared and which Booker had bought from money he had borrowed from the bank.

That was the beginning. For the next 35 years Dr. Booker T. Washington made Tuskegee a place where any determined Blacks could get a first-class education. When he retired the school consisted of more than a hundred buildings and two hundred teachers and 1500 students. Most importantly, he taught the world that, given the opportunity, Blacks **were** just as skilled in the academic field as anyone else.

Activity

To the teacher:

Prepare a small box with something inside, either valuable (a ring) or not (a paper clip) and carefully wrap it up with fancy gift wrap or just plain paper.

Tell your students to take a sheet of notebook paper and fold it vertically, turning the paper with the LEFT side up. Number from one to six. Answer the following questions either yes, no, or maybe.

1. Do you like pigeons as pets?

2. Do you like to eat raw fish?

3. Do you like classical music?

4. Would you like to live in Alaska?

5. Do you like to waltz?

6. Would you like to know what is inside this box?

Now ask your students to turn their papers over on the RIGHT side and answer the following questions either yes, no, or maybe.

1. Have you ever owned a pigeon?

2. Have you ever eaten raw fish?

3. Have you ever attended a symphony concert or listened completely through on a record?

4. Have you ever been to Alaska?

5. Do you know how to waltz?

6. Do you think there is something valuable in this box?

Activity

To the teacher:

Up to now no prior reference should be made to the fact that this activity is an indicator of prejudice. Tell your students at this point to open up their papers and score themselves on their prejudices according to the following system:

1. If the answer on the left was either yes or no and the right answer was no, then score zero.

2. If the answer on the left was either yes or no and the right answer was yes, then score one point.

3. If the answer on the left was maybe and the right answer was no, score two points.

4. If the answer on the left side was maybe and the right side was yes, then score three points.

On the box question, students get three points if they answered the right side as maybe. All other responses get zero.

Scoring:

18-15	Very open-minded
14-10	Mature approach to life and people
9-5	Prone to prejudice
4-0	Prejudiced, immature

Questions for discussion:

1. Can you tell what is inside a box by its outside appearance?

2. Can you make a valid decision about a person without knowing all about him?

3. Are people like boxes with different wrappings?

4. Do you think you are free of prejudice yourself?

5. What is a good way to overcome prejudice?

THE HUMBLE MAN WAS A KING

The Life of Martin Luther King

When the great preacher stood up to preach, his message was not primarily religious but rather one of human rights. Those listening were not of a religious sect but were bound together by a far stronger tie: that of pain and suffering. They were Blacks listening to the gospel of equality preached by one of equality's most eloquent, Martin Luther King. In reality, he was an ordained minister; his father was also an ordained minister before him. Martin had shown such promise in school that his father had wanted him to become a physician, but later the boy decided to follow his father's footsteps into the pulpit.

His first church was in Montgomery, Alabama, where he served a large black congregation. Not long after he arrived there, a black woman was arrested for sitting in the white section of a public bus. The city of Montgomery had a law, as did many southern American cities, which required all black people to sit in a section in the rear of the bus reserved especially for Blacks. Because the woman had refused she now sat in prison, charged with breaking the law.

Prominent black leaders of the city gathered to determine how they could help the situation. One of them was Martin Luther King. It was decided to persuade as many people in the black community as possible to stop using the buses. Since the majority of bus riders were black, this would mean the bus operation would immediately begin to lose a great deal of money.

Martin Luther King was designated to carry out this plan. The black community rallied behind his leadership although it meant great personal sacrifice for almost all of them. Many now had to walk long distances to work, getting up very early and returning home very late. Many black cab drivers carried black passengers for the cost of a bus fare. Month after month the campaign went on. After a year it began to look hopeless until, faced with the financial collapse of their public bus system, the city of Montgomery finally gave in and permitted the Blacks to sit where there was a vacant seat.

The fight for rights in Montgomery had gained Dr. King national status as a black leader. He travelled all over the South telling his people that they must fight for the constitutionally guaranteed rights to attend the school of their choice, buy in the shops where they wished, and eat in the restaurants they preferred. To do this they must also fight for the right to vote freely and be given the jobs they were qualified for. But, said Dr. King, they must not fight with weapons and force but must use nonviolent means, as the success in Montgomery had demonstrated. Right would make might.

He told them that they must go where they were forbidden, do what they were prohibited from doing, go to prison if necessary. If they were attacked they must not fight back but show they were willing to suffer and even die to win the basic rights for their people. In the end, he said, not force but shame would change the unjust laws and regulations.

In many ways what happened proved him right, for his followers were brutally attacked, sometimes by even the police. He himself was imprisoned many times, struck by flying rocks, and once stabbed. A bomb was exploded on his front porch, but he miraculously escaped.

The break finally came when the U.S. Supreme Court ruled that Blacks could no longer be segregated in public schools and public buildings. This was followed by other decisions to eliminate voting and job restrictions. After a hundred years, the federal government finally stepped in to enforce, with United States marshals, the rights which Abraham Lincoln had proclaimed so long ago.

Because of his work for his people, Martin Luther King was widely loved, but also he was widely hated. One day a man stepped onto a balcony with a high-powered rifle, and Dr. King gave his life because of what he believed in. He could have lived a respectable, comfortable life without becoming embroiled in race relations, but he foresook these to live hazardously and to die for his convictions, pressing on even when he was threatened, for what he knew to be right.

Activity

To the teacher:

Tell your class that we are all going to take a few minutes to think quietly about the things that are important to each one of us. After a few quiet moments, have students write down first:

(1) Family: What concerns are there with parents, brothers, sisters?

(2) School and Friends: What concerns do I have with my school, boyfriend, girlfriend, team members, schoolwork, teachers?

(3) Community Issues: What convictions do I have concerning ecology, pollution, discrimination, drug use, abortion and the draft?

(4) National: What convictions do I have on patriotism or loyalty to state or neighborhood?

(5) Personal: What convictions do I have on religion, politics or labor unions?

Have students consider each one of these factors and write down carefully those things which are deeply important to them under each of the suggested topics. Using this list, they are now ready to do the next part of this activity.

Make a ditto sheet of the following and distribute one to each student:

1. I would be willing to give up my life for _____

   _____

2. I am ready to fight with all my physical strength for _____

   _____

3. I am ready to stand up in a group and defend my beliefs in _____

   _____

4. I am in favor of, but would take no public stand on _____

   _____

5. I might share with my close friends the belief that _____

   _____

6. There are no issues I value very much because _____

   _____

For those students who have answered any one of the first three questions, give them a second sheet with these questions on it:

1. Have you ever publicly announced your position to others? When and how?

2. Have you ever actually DONE anything about your position?

3. Do you think it is likely that you will ever change your mind about your beliefs on this subject?

The teacher might now do an interview with several students who have varying degrees of convictions, trying to probe at when and how they arrived at their convictions, including a student who seems to have none. Possible interview questions:

1. In view of your convictions, what would you do if you were President of the U.S.?

2. If you could be any character in history you wished, how would you have made things differently than they are now?

3. What would the world be like if everyone in it felt the way you do?

4. What steps do you think should be taken to persuade more people to agree with your point of view?

5. Do you admire, dislike or have no feeling towards those who feel differently about this issue than you do?

The teacher should permit other members of the class to also ask interview questions, but do not encourage private debates which this activity sometimes becomes. If the class finds that an issue is controversial, it would be better to have a prepared debate on the topic at some later time when both positions can be supported with facts rather than casual opinions.

THE LADY WITH THE LAMP
The Story of Florence Nightingale (1820-1910)

Over a hundred years ago, a great war raged in a place called the Crimea. England and France sent their best young men to fight the Russians over causes that hardly justified the great loss of lives on both sides. Reports came back to England of the terrible conditions of the battlefield wounded and the hospitals. The public outcry against the lack of care for the injured soldiers became so great that the government decided to send a group of trained nurses to see if conditions could not be improved.

Thirty-eight nurses, some of them nuns, were recruited by an energetic young hospital matron named Florence Nightingale. Florence came from a wealthy family and could have easily lived a life of ease, but felt a deep responsibility to care for the ill and dying, so she refused to live an easy, aristocratic life, preferring to devote her efforts to improve the conditions among those suffering in pain and disease. She gladly responded to the challenge to serve the sick on the battlefront.

The conditions she discovered upon her arrival were far worse than she had imagined. The so-called hospital was an old, broken down building, with a leaky roof and no lights or heating. Most of the five thousand men crowded into it were lying on the ground simply bleeding to death from their wounds or dying from the cold and starvation, since there was no food. As she tried to step over the pools of blood, the dead and the dying, she finally found a doctor who, instead of tending to the sick, sat at a great table stacked high with paperwork and government forms. Florence withheld the great storm that arose within her from the dreadful sight she encountered, and quietly but very forcefully mobilized the group of nurses into action. They often worked twenty hours a day, catching naps for moments here and there as they cleaned, clothed, and cared for the wounded.

Still the wounded flooded in. Florence demanded another ward to relieve the already overcrowded wards, more food and blankets, and repair of sanitation facilities. She was immediately surrounded by a wave of opposition from doctors, army officers, politicians and petty, jealous people who accused her of being bossy and overbearing, interested only in her own authority. In her letters home, Florence told how all these accusations and criticisms hurt her deeply, but how they faded away when she stepped into a ward of wounded soldiers. They adored her. They knew how bad conditions were before she had come. Every night she toured between the cots with lamp in hand, with a soft word or gentle touch for each of the suffering. They soon began to call her the "lady with the lamp."

When the wounded recovered, they went back home and proclaimed how she had saved their lives, and soon the government sent another group of nurses to join her. As the battles raged on, she went to the battle area herself to improve field care for the wounded. Exhausted from working long hours, she contracted a fever and had to be carried back to the hospital where she lay weak and helpless for many weeks.

Finally, the war was over and Florence returned back home to England. To her amazement, she was greeted as a heroine. The Queen wanted to give her a medal and everyone in London wanted to see her and thank her for what she had done. She was grateful to them, but said she wished only to live quietly with her parents in the country.

She spent the rest of her life training nurses and sending medical teams all over the world to improve the conditions of those confined to hospitals. If you ever go to a hospital, you will enjoy good nursing care partly because Florence Nightingale chose to help sick people instead of living a carefree life of luxury and ease.

Activity

To the teacher:

Read the following story to your class or make a ditto sheet and distribute copies for them to read. If you make a ditto sheet include the questions in sections I, II, and III. Have your students write their answers to sections I and II. On section III divide the class into teams of five or six, depending on the size of your class, and assign each team to report on one question with reasons for their answers. Permit the rest of the class to interview them about how they arrived at their conclusions. Look for contradictions in their previously stated values.

The Doctor's Advice

John sat in his cell. Down the hall he could hear the measured tread of guards coming to get him. Now the key was rattling in the lock of his barred door.

He was too weak to move. Would they beat him again? His ragged uniform reminded him of the proud officer he once was before his capture. He looked at his battered hands, swollen, black and blue, wondering what his face must look like under the stubble of an unshaven beard, marked with cuts and bruises.

The guards roughly yanked him to his feet. He was surprised he could still stand after all the days and nights without sleep. What day was this? He looked automatically at his wrist, but his watch had long since been taken.

Down the hallway he stumbled toward that brightly lighted room with its single chair under the floodlights and its faceless voice asking always the same question: "Will you now ask your men to join our program of political enlightenment?"

Why did they bother to ask him? They had the power to force their prisoners to do anything they wished, yet John knew with his order many men would cease to resist, saying: "My superior officer told me to do it."

Soon he would be dead and it wouldn't matter anyway. He knew with his wounds and his present treatment, he couldn't last much longer.

To his surprise, the guards stopped at the door rather than take him in. He couldn't see with the glaring lights. Instead he heard a soft, friendly voice saying: "There's no need to go back in there again. I'm a doctor. I've come to take care of you. Sign this silly order you have been asked to sign, so I can help you."

What would you have done?

I. a. Would you have signed the order in an effort to save your life?

 b. Would you have stalled for time by asking to get cleaned up and rested before you appeared before your men?

 c. Would you have continued to refuse and thus become a symbol of bravery for your men?

 d. Would you have asked to talk to a representative of the International Red Cross, so he could advise you?

 e. Would you have taken some other course of action?

II. On the basis of your decision, describe the effect upon:

 a. Your captors, and their further treatment of you.

 b. Your men and their attitude toward you.

 c. Your men and their attitude toward their captors.

 d. Your family back home when they discover the truth.

 e. The armed forces of the United States, which you represent.

III. a. Do you think captured enemy soldiers should be forced to take a program telling them the cause they were fighting for was wrong?

 b. Should prisoners, during wartime, be subjected to torture in order to gain information that would speed the victory?

 c. What do you think of the statement: "Every man has his breaking point"?

 d. Is it possible to commit a "crime" against an enemy during wartime?

 e. What do you think of General MacArthur's statement: "In war, there is no substitute for victory"?

GO PLACIDLY

Dated 1692 and found in a church in Baltimore, Maryland

Go placidly amid the noise and haste, and remember what peace there may be in silence. As far as possible without surrender, be on good terms with all persons. Speak your truth quietly and clearly and listen to others, even the dull and ignorant; they too have their stories.

Avoid loud and aggressive persons; they are vexations to the spirit. If you compare yourself with others, you may become vain and bitter; for always there will be greater and lesser persons than yourself. Enjoy your achievements as well as your plans.

Keep interested in your own career, however humble; it is a real possession in the changing fortunes of time. Exercise caution in your business affairs; for the world is full of trickery. But let this not blind you to what virtue there is; many persons strive for high ideals; and everywhere life is full of heroism.

Be yourself. Especially do not feign affection. Neither be cynical about love; for in the face of all aridity and disenchantment, it is perennial as the grass.

Take kindly to counsel of the years, gracefully surrendering the things of youth. Nurture strength of spirit to shield you in sudden misfortune. But do not distress yourself with imaginings. Many fears are born of fatigue and loneliness. Beyond a wholesome discipline, be gentle with yourself.

You are a child of the universe, no less than the trees and the stars; you have a right to be here. And whether or not it is clear to you, no doubt the universe is unfolding as it should.

Therefore be at peace with God, whatever you conceive him to be, and whatever your labours and aspirations, in the noisy confusion of life keep peace with your soul.

Be careful; strive to be happy. With all its sham, drudgery, and broken dreams, it is still a beautiful world.

Activity

To the teacher:

Tell each student to draw a horizontal line across a sheet of notebook paper turned lengthwise. At the left end of the line put his date of birth; at the other end of the line put today's date and his present age. Now have the student divide the line into approximately equal spaces representing the years of his life.

Tell students to think back as far as they can remember and mark their lifelines with the following indicators:

1. Put a star (*) on the line at the approximate date for the happiest moments they can think of (Christmas, birthdays, holidays, getting something important, trips, special visitors, programs, special events, successes).

After each star turn the page sideways and write a brief note telling about the happy event.

2. Put a check on the line for the unhappy times (think of accidents, illnesses, failures, family problems, punishments, deaths, loss of pets, losses, moving, etc.). Again write a brief note about each.

3. Put an X for the following:

    a. The times you have moved to different places (add a note telling when and where)

    b. The different schools you have attended

    c. When you got various pets (note kind and name); the dates of their deaths

    d. When your family got a new car (note the make)

40

4. Think about the best friends you have had in your life right up to now. Put a circle on the line for about the time when you met and a circle with an X for about the time that you drifted apart (write a note after each symbol).

5. Make a triangle for the most important event in your life. Put this around an existing symbol if you have listed it already.

Now redraw your lifeline in the space below, and the one you have just completed, only now make the line go up and down for the high and low points. For the neutral events, leave the line in the middle. Your lifeline should be jagged, like this:

Questions:

1. Is your lifeline mostly up or mostly down?

2. Does it end up or end down?

3. Can you see any pattern in your life so far?

4. Predict where your lifeline will go in the next five years.

The teacher should urge several of the students to share their lifelines with the class.

41

THE FIRST AND THE LAST PORTRAIT

The Legend of Leonardo da Vinci's Masterpiece: *The Last Supper*

Many years ago the devout monks in a large monastery in Italy commissioned one of the greatest artists who ever lived to paint a picture of Jesus with His disciples in their last supper together before His crucifixion. The artist was Leonardo da Vinci, and it turned out to be his greatest masterpiece, showing Jesus with His head framed by an open window surrounded on either side by the faithful twelve.

The painting reflects the artist's obsession for detail and perspective, but it does not indicate the many years it required for him to finish it. Leonardo thought he would begin the tableau with the central figure of Jesus, so he began his search for a model who would show Jesus as he imagined Him to be: the kindest, noblest human being the world had ever seen. Each day Leonardo wandered the streets peering at the passersby, searching for the face which would show the humility and yet the majesty he wished to paint. Weeks turned into months; then one day on a busy street he saw the man whose face displayed all the qualities he had been searching for. The young man was more than pleased to pose for the great artist and after several weeks at the monastery, he was paid by Leonardo and went on his way.

Next came each one of the apostles. Many sketches were made of each man until the artist had clearly decided upon the features which he felt characterized each personality.

Then again the search began to find a live model which best exemplified these characteristics. As the time went by, many of the monks began to feel that the painting would never be completed since Leonardo was also very busy as a sculptor, engineer and architect.

Slowly, after many years, the painting neared completion. Only one figure was left to paint; it was that of Judas Iscariot, the only non-Galilean of the apostles, the traitor who had betrayed Jesus to His enemies. Again Leonardo set out to find his model with his usual discrimination and persistence. First, he visited the prisons, but none of the criminals bore the look of greed and treachery he was looking for. Then he toured the drinking halls and the gambling dens, but these men did not show the inner wickedness the artist was looking for.

Then, in the city of Florence, he finally found him in a dirty wine house cellar. As the artist talked with the man, he was even more assured he had never seen such an evil expression on a man's face, an expression which lighted up only slightly when he was offered a small fee to pose for Leonardo.

Back at the monastery, Leonardo carefully seated his model to take full advantage of the light, then picked up his brushes and began the master strokes that would complete his painting. He had only begun when, as he glanced over his shoulder to study the man's face, he saw great tears rolling down his cheeks.

"What is the matter?" inquired the painter.

The sad, bent model began haltingly, "Many years ago I came to this same monastery to pose for another picture. You had chosen me to portray Jesus. Since then I have lived a wicked, miserable life and now I am your idea of Judas. That is enough to make even a man like me to weep."

Activity

To the teacher:

Divide your class into groups of no more than twelve or fifteen. Have them sit down on the floor in a circle with the lights out and the shades drawn. You should now join them with a lighted candle in your hand.

Tell them we are going to imagine that we are all trapped in a damaged submarine at the bottom of the ocean. All the electricity is out. We must make our escape to the surface one by one through the pressure hatch. This will take time and our air is running out. Only the first few will make it.

Each person will take the candle and tell why he should be included in the first few to go. He should tell what good things he has to give to the world and what plans he has for his life, or how much others need him or whatever reasons he feels are important for him to be a survivor.

The teacher should try to keep the mood serious by going first and telling the class why he thinks he should be a survivor. After he has done so, he should pass the candle on to a verbal student who will speak next and so set the pattern on around the circle. After everyone has spoken, take a vote to determine which four will go first.

Questions:

1. Why did you have a hard time telling the good things about yourself?

2. Do you think that the person who said nothing or very little should be left behind? Why?

3. Have you ever thought of your life plans before, or are you just living with no objectives?

4. Do you think that people who are burdens to society should be kept alive at the taxpayers' expense?

5. Would you be willing to donate your heart to some important person in government or science to keep him alive? How about a movie star? A popular musician? (Look for contradictions from those who said very little.)

6. If someone close to you told you he was going to commit suicide, what would you say to him?

44

THE MAN WHO HELPED OTHERS LIVE A CLEAN LIFE
The Story of Samuel Colgate

A young sixteen-year-old country boy left his hometown in upper New York State one day to seek his fortune in the big city. In those days there were few railroads and hardly any roads that led directly to the big city, so Sam started walking along the canal which he knew eventually would take him to his destination. After a while, he came to a set of locks through which all the canal boats had to pass. One of the boat captains was having difficulty with the lockmaster because of the horses used to pull the boat along. Sam, who was a farm boy, knew all about horses, so he stepped in and gave a hand with the horses while the boat passed through the locks.

"Say, young man, you sure know how to handle a team!" exclaimed the captain.

"Glad to help. Wonder if you might need some help on your way down to New York?"

"Sure would. Come on aboard."

For the the next few weeks, Sam worked hard each day with the team on the bank, pulling the boat along the canal. One evening after they had eaten supper, the captain said, "Sam, you're a hard worker. What are you going to do when you get to New York?"

"Well, I don't have any idea, really."

"Spill out your pockets for me, Sam."

"My pockets? What for?"

"Don't ask questions, boy, just do it. I'm the captain, you know."

Sam emptied his pockets on the deck. Out spilled a piece of candle and a white lump, some coins and a pocket knife. The captain picked up the white lump, saying, "What's this?"

"Oh, that's just some soap I helped to make before I left home. Mom wanted me to wash regular, so I took some with me."

"You know how to make soap?"

"Yes, sir. Don't everybody?"

"Sam, I'm going to give you a bit of advice besides just a boat ride. No, not everybody knows how to make soap, and it's something that everyone needs and uses up so they have to buy more. Somebody in this world is going to make soap, and it might as well be you. But let me tell you, Sam, it takes more than just knowing how. You have to give people a full pound of honest soap for their money so they keep coming back to buy from you. You follow my advice, and you'll be a rich man some day."

Samuel Colgate never forgot the words of that canal boat captain. In later years he had them engraved and mounted in his office in one of the largest companies in the world, because Samuel Colgate's toothpaste and soap are probably the most famous in the world. Maybe you have tried them yourself. But Sam Colgate did not keep all his money to himself. After his family was educated and gone, he gave all the income from his giant operation to charity in order to help others who were not as fortunate as he had been.

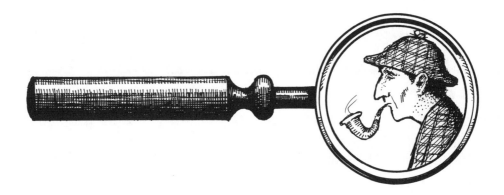

Activity

To the teacher:

Tell your students that today we are all going to play detective. Have them choose a partner so the class is divided into pairs.

The partner who has a birthday closest to August 19 (Sherlock Holmes' birthday) will act as the detective. The other person will now give the detective his wallet, purse or notebook for him to carefully examine its contents.

From these personal possessions, the detective must now write a statement describing that person's characteristics, including age, sex, weight, height, color of eyes, etc.; a description of his activities, interests; and what the detective feels is the most important thing in his life. The teacher should go first. Have one of your better students examine your wallet or purse and do a description of you from the contents. It's always fun to purposely slip in something humorous like a shrunken head or CIA identity card.

The game usually turns out to be much fun since the detective can reach erroneous conclusions about the character of the person he is investigating just based on the belongings he carries with him every day. If the student has only a notebook with him, the investigator should examine what he has written on it as a clue to his character in addition to what is in it.

Have several of the detectives report their findings; then reverse the roles with the detective becoming the suspect and vice versa.

Questions for discussion:

1. Were there things in your wallet, purse, notebook that you would rather not share with others?

2. Did you ask your detective (were you asked) not to mention a particular item?

3. Do you think that the things we carry around with us every day REALLY say something about us?

4. If there were a computer someplace (and there probably is), which has recorded all the information about you, what kinds of information would you NOT want to be on record?

HAPPINESS MUST BE IMPORTANT BECAUSE EVERYONE IS LOOKING FOR IT

Happiness must be important because everyone is looking for it. If you were to stop the average man on the street and ask him if he wanted to be happy, he probably would look at you as though you were a little crazy, because everyone wants to be happy and everyone seems to be looking for happiness. The unfortunate thing is the average man on the street, if you were to talk to him, would tell you that he's not very happy. He is really quite miserable even though he lives in this beautiful, wonderful country of America.

A long, long time ago, thousands of years ago, there lived a very famous king whose name was Solomon. He decided one day since he was unhappy, that he would go on a quest to try to find happiness.

The first thing he did was to turn to alcohol and wine. He found when he drank a lot of wine it made him happy for a few minutes, but then he began to do foolish things, and people thought he was a very silly person.

Then he decided he would put up very beautiful public buildings and put his name on the fronts of them. After he had built a lot of beautiful buildings he found these did not bring him happiness either.

Next he decided he would plant a marvelous, beautiful garden and grow many trees. He looked out on his wonderful garden one day, and he found this didn't bring him very much happiness either.

Since he was a very rich king, he asked his servants to bring him all of his gold and silver so he could sit down and admire the gold, silver, and precious jewels he owned. He found riches didn't make him very happy either.

He then called for all his musicians, his singers and his magicians to entertain him, but after a while he got bored listening to them.

He thought perhaps he would find happiness in sexual pleasure. So he had many hundreds of different women from all over the world come and marry him. But he soon got tired of his wives also after awhile.

He never was able to find true happiness. He wrote a book called Ecclesiastes, in which at the end of the book, telling about his experiences, he said, "Vanity, vanity, all is vanity. The only thing that counts is to fear God and give service to others."

How do people try to find happiness today? Many people do the same things Solomon did. Young people would like to have new things, new cars or new hi-fi sets, or new clothes. Adults find that they would like to have new homes, fancy big cars, swimming pools, or new boats. They discover, as Solomon did, none of these things seems to bring lasting happiness. They discover they are still restless and discontented just as Solomon was.

A very famous philosopher, John Stewart Mill, once said, "I have learned to seek my happiness by limiting my desires rather than in attempting to satisfy my desires." People who are always wanting something else are the people who are the most unhappy. So to find happiness, if we are to take the advice of others who have spent their lifetimes looking for it, we should limit our desires and find ways to give service to other people. We actually **get** by **giving**, not by wanting everything there is available, but by limiting our desires so we will be happy with what we have.

Activity

To the teacher:

Make a ditto of the following and have the students score themselves on their happiness inventory.

My Happiness Inventory

Section A—Basic Things I GET

1. Fact: Over 742 million people in the world are now judged by the UN as hungry or starving.

    Do I have plenty of different kinds of food to eat?
    Yes ___ No ___

2. Fact: Over 478 million people in the world (more than all the people in the U.S.) do not have a permanent weatherproof shelter to live in.

    Do I have a permanent home to live in?
    Yes ___ No ___

3. Fact: Only 1 out of 7250 people (about 10 times the number of students in the average school) in the world has a TV to watch.

    Do I have a TV to entertain me?
    Yes ___ No ___

4. Fact: Over 834 million people in the world have only one set of clothes to wear. Many more have no shoes, no coat, no underwear.

    Do I have enough different kinds of clothes to wear?
    Yes ___ No ___

5. Fact: Over 742 million people in the world die every year because of lack of medical care.

    When I get sick, is there a doctor and medicine to help me get well?
    Yes ___ No ___

6. Fact: Only 1 out of 8055 people in the world (about 12 times the number of students in the average school) has a refrigerator and stove in the home.

    Is there a refrigerator for cooling and a stove for cooking in my home?
    Yes ___ No ___

7. Fact: Over 451 million people in the world do not own a radio or hi-fi set.

    Are there several radios or hi-fi sets in my home?
    Yes ___ No ___

8. Fact: Only 1 out of 760 children in the world (about the number of ALL the children in the average school) has the chance to learn to read and write and calculate.

   Do I have a chance to learn to read, write and learn about numbers?
   Yes ___ No ___

9. Fact: Only 1 out of 758 million people in this world has hot and cold running water and an indoor private bathroom in the home.

   Do I have hot and cold running water and an indoor bathroom in my home?
   Yes ___ No ___

10. Fact: Over 957 million people in the world have no restaurants of any kind available to them.

   Is there a McDonald's or other kind of restaurant in my community?
   Yes___ No ___

Section B—How Much Do I GIVE in Consideration of Others? Be Honest!

1. If I OPEN it, do I CLOSE it? Yes ___ No ___ Maybe ___

2. If I turn it ON, do I turn it OFF? Yes ___ No ___ Maybe ___

3. If I UNLOCK it, then do I LOCK it? Yes ___ No ___ Maybe ___

4. If I BREAK it, do I REPAIR it? Yes ___ No ___ Maybe ___

5. If I cannot FIX it, do I REPORT it? Yes ___ No ___ Maybe ___

6. If I BORROW it, do I RETURN it? Yes ___ No ___ Maybe ___

7. If I make a MESS, do I CLEAN it up? Yes ___ No ___ Maybe ___

8. If I MOVE it, do I PUT IT BACK? Yes ___ No ___ Maybe ___

9. If I don't know HOW to run it, do I LEAVE it alone? Yes ___ No ___ Maybe ___

10. If it BELONGS to someone else, do I get PERMISSION first? Yes ___ No ___ Maybe ___

Score: 1 point for each yes in Section A; 1 point for each yes in Section B; ½ point for each maybe. Subtract score of B from A. If 5 or more, you need to look at your personal habits.

MY GOOD NAME
(My name identifies me!)

Mr. COOK

An old proverb says, "A good name is rather to be chosen than great riches." Each of us has a name that has been passed along for many, many generations. Your great, great, great, great grandfather on your daddy's side had the same last name you have.

If we have a good name, then we are proud of it. If it's not, then we can make a good name so people will respect us.

Until about 700 years ago, in the days of King Richard the Lion-Heart, most people went by a single name only. They had no second name. Sometimes the name of the city was added for some identification, such as Augustine of Canterbury or William of Locksley. After that, about 1750, a surname was added so that people had two names instead of one.

Today there are millions of people in the world who have three names: a first name, a middle name, and a last name. At the rate our population is growing, 100 years from now, it may be necessary for us to have four names to be identified.

Can you guess what the most common names are today? Perhaps if you open a telephone book, you might be able to flip through and find the most common name. You may have guessed that the most common name in America is Smith, followed by Johnson, Williams, Jones, Brown, Miller, Davis, Anderson, Wilson, Thompson, in that order. This is told to us by the government which has made a compilation of over 29 million different names passing through its computers.

There are many names that are hard to pronounce and even more difficult to spell. Some people have names they don't like because of these reasons, or because they just don't like the sounds of their names. If that's the case, it is possible to change your name if you don't like it. You can go to a court of law, show the judge you have a good reason, and the court will change your name legally to whatever name you would like it to be. Whatever name we have we shouldn't be ashamed of it.

During World War II General Montgomery was listening to the morning roll call of one of his desert tank battalions when he heard the name Guy Fawkes called. He ordered the man to step forward. He was a handsome young tank driver. The general said to the young man, "Change your name, brother soldier. You're too respectable to bear the name of a traitor."

The young man replied, "But what name shall I take, sir?"

"Take any other name; take mine if you wish," said the general.

The young soldier had his name changed on the army rolls to Bernard Law Montgomery and was known by that name until he was later killed in action.

Probably one of the greatest and most respected names of the twentieth century is Winston Churchill. After World War II was over, a worldwide banking company came to Churchill and offered him shares of stock worth many millions just for the privilege of using his name in the company's title.

Sir Winston quickly replied, "I do not wish your money. Such as it is, my name is not for sale."

If your name has a proud tradition, do your best to live up to it. If you have a name that you are not sure has some kind of tradition, make it a good one so that others in time to come will want to live up to it.

Winston S. Churchill

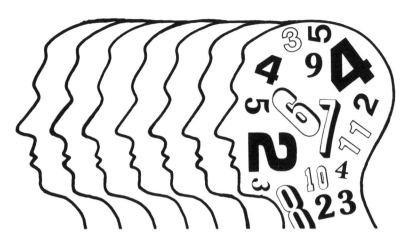

Activity

To the teacher:

Here is a fascinating activity for those students who are good with numbers, and a quick review for those who are not. Read the following to your class:

In the year 1751, Benjamin Franklin, in his publication *Poor Richard's Almanac*, showed how to figure out how many family members you had 25 generations ago, or about 900 years ago, when people first began to have a second family name.

He did it this way:
Your father and mother . . . . .2, 1st generation
Your grandfather and grandmother . . . . .4, 2nd generation
Your great grandfather and great grandmother . . . . . .8, 3rd generation

What is happening in this number sequence? (2, 4, 8, etc. It is doubling.)

What is the next number for your great, great, grandfather and grandmother? (16)

Make a table which looks like this (put on the board):

Generations:	1	2	3	4	5	6	7	8	9	10	11	12	13	14	15	16	17	18	19	20	21	22	23	24
Ancestors:	2	4	8	16	32																			

Can you figure out how many ancestors you have going back 900 years?

($2^{25} = 33,554,432$—over 33 million!)

For those students who are better with words than they are with numbers, ask them to write down their first, middle and last names. Tell them to rearrange the letters to make several words that describe themselves. Typical words might be: *hard, work, play, talk, love, home, car, tender, fear, sick, self, me, hate, party, weak, poor, rich, happy, boy, girl, tired,* etc.

The teacher should go first by putting his or her name on the board and, with the help of the class, make several words that fit the teacher (try *smart, easy, good,* etc.).

A BRAND-NEW LABEL

(A true story of Old England)

Two young boys lived in a rural English village many years ago. One day they were caught stealing. They faithfully promised the magistrate that they would never steal again. As they got older they thought they could take more valuable things and get away with it. As they were passing a neighbor's farm, James said, "Look! Isn't that a new set of lambs? We could get a gold coin for that pair in the next village."

Silently, they slipped into the enclosure and soon were on their way, each with a small lamb under his arm. Unknown to them, however, they had been seen and instead of gold coins a constable was waiting for them at the next village. This time, the magistrate was not to be put off with promises. He ordered them branded. This was a popular method of punishment which had a double effect. Not only was it painful for the guilty party, but it also notified the world to beware of the law-breaker. Thus, a red hot iron with the letters ST for "sheep thief" was pressed to the young men's foreheads to imprint them for the rest of their lives.

Sadly, the brothers nursed their wounds. "I think I will go away to a far-off land," said James, "to someplace where no one knows me. I could not face all the people who know me the rest of my life with this mark on my forehead."

"Yes, it will be difficult," agreed his brother, "but we brought it on ourselves. We can't blame anyone else. Maybe if we try hard enough, people will eventually forgive us for what we've done."

"With this brand on us? Not likely! We will always be laughed at and mistrusted. I'm going someplace where at least I can start over again." With that he gathered up all his belongings, shook hands with his brother and left the village.

He journeyed on till he found another village in a foreign country. There he tried to find work but could not speak the language very well, nor did he have a skill to offer a prospective employer. The ugly brand on his forehead disfigured his appearance, although people did not understand what the letters meant. Unable to work, he moved aimlessly from village to village and from town to town, a penniless vagabond. Finally, one winter he was found frozen to death and put into an unmarked grave, for no one in that country knew his name.

His brother grimly had made up his mind to return to the village and try to make amends for the wrong he had done. It was very difficult. Small children would follow after him jeering and calling, "Thief! Thief!" while throwing mud and sticks. No one would speak to him or have any dealing with him in any way. He kept alive by cutting wood from the forest and selling it wherever he could.

Slowly, the villagers began to realize that he always gave an honest measure of wood for his charge, and he made a real attempt to supply everyone, even when it was cold and icy. One very cold winter it was only his steady stock of wood that kept two old widows from freezing to death, although one of them could not afford to pay him. From then on, everyone came to love and trust him.

Years later a stranger came to the village and he stopped a young child playing in the street. "Could you please tell me what those letters ST mean on the forehead of that old man?"

"Oh, yes, sir. You must be new around here. That's the nicest, most wonderful man in our village. Those letters are ST, short for *saint*."

Note to the teacher: The true story of "A Brand-New Label" applies to all of us, for we all wear labels of one sort or another. Each one of us wears the label of his personality which we can no more discard than these brothers could get rid of their brands.

The following activity is designed to help young people "put their best foot forward" when they meet others and how best to wear the label of their personalities when interacting in a group.

Activity

To the teacher:
Distribute a 3″ x 5″ file card with a pin to each student.

1. In the middle of each card, have the student print the name or nickname he likes to be called in bold, large letters.

2. In the upper right-hand corner, the student should print: "My favorite food is . . . . " Each student should then print in his favorite dish.

3. In the lower right-hand corner, the student should print: "The day I'm looking forward to is . . . ." Here he might put graduation day, the day I get married, the day I graduate from college, etc.

4. In the upper left-hand corner, the student should print: "I am good at . . . ." Possibilities here are reading, sports, hoping, eating, studying, playing the guitar, etc. He might list several.

5. In the lower left-hand corner, the student should print: "I am interested in . . . ." Hobbies and special activities should be listed here, such as swimming, running, music, drawing, sewing, gardening, etc. List several.

I am good at_____   My favorite food is
_____   _____
_____   _____

                        NAME OR
                        NICKNAME

I am interested in_____   The day I am looking
_____   forward to is_____
_____   _____

Tell your students to pin their cards on themselves; then have them move around the room, shaking hands and meeting everyone else and reading everyone else's card. The teacher should join in, setting the example. Tell them that this is a game on how to meet other people and talk to new acquaintances.

They should find someone else who has the same thing written on his card for the next part of the game.

After they have met and read everyone else's card, have them sit together with the person who has something on his/her card which matches his own. The teacher should make sure everyone is paired up; if the class has an odd number of students, the teacher can pair up with the extra student.

After they have paired up, have each one stand and introduce his partner, using the name card and whatever other information he has discovered about his new friend. The teacher should begin the introductions with her own partner.

Questions for discussion:

1. When you shook hands with others, did they look you straight in the eye, or did they look away and feebly take your hand? Which kind of person gives you the best impression?

2. (The teacher should select some distinctive article of clothing for this question.) "One person today is wearing . . . . Who is it?"

3. When you meet new people, is it wise to talk about yourself or to talk about the other person?

4. Did you find it easier to meet people of your same sex or the opposite sex? Why? How can you overcome being self-conscious?

5. Is it easier to meet people who have the same interests you do, or is it more interesting to meet people with different interests?

6. When you introduce someone to a group, what are the important things you should mention?

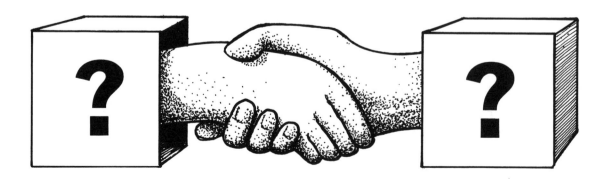

THE FINAL STRETCH

John slipped on his brightly colored helmet, pulled his goggles down and his muffler up over his nose and mouth. The gentle purr of the mighty engine behind him immediately exploded into a deafening roar as he depressed the accelerator with a few quick thrusts. All drivers' eyes were riveted on the starter's flag as it waved gently in anticipation. Suddenly it dropped. Almost simultaneously, the air filled with the screams of burning rubber, the roar of engines and the blue smoke of exhaust fumes.

The hundreds of horsepower deep within John's car made the sleek mechanical beast lurch forward as John sped toward the first turn. Wheel to wheel with those next to him, John kept his foot flat on the accelerator and his eye on the distant bend. Approaching the curve, he figured he might have a lead of a few inches, not more than a foot. He flung the great car into the turn full speed with tires screeching as it slipped sideways under the momentum of such great speed. Around the turn, John deftly, carefully straightened the car into the backstretch. He was away, clearly in the lead. Behind him the mirror played out the drama of the pack as other drivers sought to gain advantageous positions for the remainder of the race. Ahead of him lay a clear empty track flashing by him at an incredible speed that blurred all except distant objects. No jockeying for position, no nervous stress of hairbreadth decisions; he was in the lead!

Lap after lap sped by: the pits, the stands, the backstretch. No one could catch him now. The flag and cheering of the crowd signaled the final circuit. Just one more lap; all he had to do was keep his head and drive carefully across that finish line.

He carefully threaded his way between several cars who were a couple of laps behind him as he rounded the final curve toward the homestretch. Over beyond them he could see the checked flag in the distance. With nothing ahead but victory, he pressed down on the accelerator. The throat of the mighty engine cried out and then coughed in a dreadful choking sound and then died completely. Vainly he pumped the accelerator, but the only sound was the whistle of the wind as the great car's high friction tires caused the speedometer to plumet to zero.

59

The cold realization of disappointment swept through him. After leading all the way he now was going to lose the race. "No! I'm going to finish!" He quickly steered the car to the outer lane away from passing cars. Snapping off his seat belt, he leaped out of the cockpit onto the pavement and began pushing the car while it was still gently rolling. Now the massive engine became an enemy; it took every ounce of strength to heave its great weight forward. Other cars zipped by him but he kept on. All the cars had passed him now, but still a deafening noise filled the air. As he turned he saw all the people in the stands cheering and clapping and waving him on.

The Finish Official stood smiling patiently with the checked flag John had seen seemingly so long ago. The blisters on his hands stung, the hot pavement burned through his thin driving shoes, the pain in his chest stabbed as he gasped for breath, but down inside John no longer felt disappointed.

He lost the race, but now he realized that he had won something more important: his self-respect.

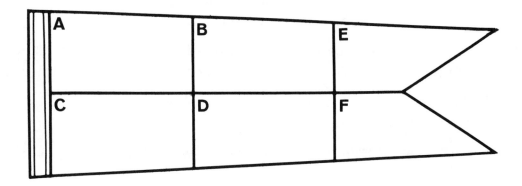

Activity

To the teacher:

After you have read the story to the students, show them an example of a family coat of arms, if you have one. Discuss the historical significance of these symbols of family importance. Tell how flags often represent personal standards.

1. Distribute copies of the above illustration, or have the students draw their own on sheets of paper.

2. Then ask your students to draw, in the appropriate spaces, sketches of ideas that answer the following questions. Emphasize that artwork doesn't count. Drawings should just roughly represent what the student has in mind.

In the appropriate spaces draw:

    a. Something about which you would never change your mind.

    b. Something you are trying to become in the future.

    c. One thing you would like to do before you are old.

    d. Things you are good at.

    e. A personal motto you live by.

    f. Organizations you belong to.

If a student is not sure about any of the above, just have him leave that space blank.

After they have finished, have your students share their drawings, telling others what they mean. Post them around the room and hold a gallery walk, having each student tell about his personal flag.

1000 DAYS AND 1001 NIGHTS
The Story of Scheherezade

In Baghdad the king is called the Caliph, and he has absolute power of life and death over all of his subjects. It was little wonder that all those in the court trembled with fear as the Caliph stormed about in a great rage.

"Traitor! Unfaithful plotter!"

One of the courtiers whispered to his friend, "What is this that so greatly has distraught our great Caliph?"

"It is his wife. I should say, it **was** his wife. He had her beheaded this morning after he discovered that she had been plotting with one of the ministers to poison him."

The Caliph's shouts and angry curses echoed down the hall as he strode from the courtroom. "Send me the First Minister!" he ordered.

"You called for me, Most High Caliph?"

"Summon together the beautiful women of my court, for tonight I shall remarry."

"Tonight? But don't you find it difficult to remarry so soon?"

"I do not trust any woman. They are all treacherous and untrustworthy; so I shall marry a different one each day from this day forth and then have her put to death the next day."

"But, Your Majesty," pleaded the First Minister. "You may live many years. Are you going to execute one of the beautiful maidens of our land each day? Is it wise or just to seek revenge on the innocent girls of our land because of the infidelity of one?"

"You insolent dog! How dare you question my commands! I shall begin with **your** eldest daughter. What is her name?"

"Scheherezade, Oh Great Caliph, but she is too young to marry."

"Bring her ready for the wedding tomorrow or I shall behead your entire household and burn your home to the ground!" The Caliph then grinned a twisted smile. "Tell her she will be a queen . . . for one day, that is."

The First Minister's heart sank as he went home to tell his beloved daughter, but to his surprise, she took the news quite calmly.

"Don't worry, Father. Just ask permission to bring my little sister, Dunyashad, to the palace for the wedding."

The minister was a little puzzled at this, but assured her he would. The next day was filled with singing and feasting. As darkness fell, the guests gathered in the king's private chamber to bid him good night.

"Please sit down everyone," said the new queen. "It is the custom in my family to tell my sister a bedtime story. Since you are all our guests, you may stay and listen."

Scheherezade then unfolded before them a fascinating tale of the magic flying horse. All sat hypnotized, gripped with stirring adventure for the great winged beast. Just as she reached the climax of the story, the hall echoed with the twelve strokes of midnight.

"I shall have to finish my story tomorrow night," said the bride, "for I know that the Caliph has ordered all to retire at midnight."

For a moment the Caliph was angered, for he had planned her death in the morning. Then he said grudgingly, "All right, you may all return tomorrow night." He had become so interested that he thought he would like to hear what happened himself. Besides one more night wouldn't make that much difference, he told himself.

But the next night, Scheherezade began the tale of Sinbad, the sea rover, an even more captivating story, masterfully told by the young queen. Again at midnight, she reached a most thrilling part of the adventure and again the Caliph granted her one more night to continue. This went on night after night, each time the story reaching its climactic point at the midnight hour, each night the king granting her one more day to live.

In the meantime, Scheherezade lived up to queenly responsibilities in every way. She was gentle and kind to princes and beggers alike, she gave money to feed the poor and to house the sick, and she cared tenderly for her husband in every way.

Finally, on the one thousand and first night, she surveyed everyone. At midnight her story ended. Everyone sat in uneasy silence for they thought surely that the Caliph would now carry out his death sentence.

He rose slowly and came over to her side and took her hand. "I love you, dear Scheherezade. I would as soon die myself as to see any harm come to you. You have taught me to love when I was filled with hate and revenge. My only wish is to love you and live together a long and happy life."

This story ends as Scheherezade ended all her stories: "They lived happily ever after."

Activity

To the teacher:

Have your students fold a piece of notebook paper vertically and answer the following statements either true or false.

How Much Do You Know About the Other Sex?

1. Husband/Wife arguments are usually won by the spouse who does the most talking.
   TRUE   FALSE

2. Women are better at solving complicated problems than men.   TRUE   FALSE

3. Men get along on less sleep than women.   TRUE   FALSE

4. When faced with a severe crisis, a woman is more likely to go to pieces than a man.
   TRUE   FALSE

5. Men are fussier about their food.   TRUE   FALSE

6. Men tend to be more self-centered than women.   TRUE   FALSE

7. When a couple has mother-in-law trouble, it's usually the wife's mother who is to blame.   TRUE   FALSE

8. Women talk more about men than men talk about women.   TRUE   FALSE

9. Wives understand their husbands better than husbands understand their wives.
   TRUE   FALSE

10. Women make more fuss about minor or nonexistent ailments.   TRUE   FALSE

11. Men are more truthful than women.   TRUE   FALSE

12. Most husbands are more intelligent than their wives.   TRUE   FALSE

13. Divorced men are better risks for a second marriage than divorced women.
    TRUE   FALSE

14. The widespread belief that women are more talkative than men actually has no basis in fact.   TRUE   FALSE

15. Men have a greater capacity for happiness than women.   TRUE   FALSE

Take a consensus on the answer to each question and permit your class to discuss each answer before reading them the following correct responses.

1. TRUE. Harvard University studies show that when domestic differences arise it's the spouse that does the most talking who gets his or her way.

2. FALSE. A study at Stanford University has shown that men are as much as 50 percent more proficient than women at problem solving.

3. TRUE. Medical authorities find that women need more sleep.

4. FALSE. Studies show that in a real crisis, a woman is much more likely to remain calm than a man.

5. FALSE. Dietetic studies show that women are far more finicky about what they eat than men.

6. FALSE. Psychologists have found that women are far more self-centered than men. They have fewer outside interests.

7. FALSE. The Institute of Family Relations has discovered that it usually is the husband's mother who is the troublemaker.

8. TRUE. The University of Minnesota found that women talk far more about men than vice versa.

9. FALSE. The Veterans Administration discovered that husbands have a far better insight into their wives character than vice versa.

10. TRUE. Cornell University Medical School found that women tend to exaggerate almost all types of complaints and ailments.

11. FALSE. Psychological tests at De Paul University showed that when it came to outright lies, men led the field.

12. TRUE. Studies show that women tend to be attracted to men they can look up to intellectually and vice versa.

13. FALSE. Sociological studies done at U.S.C. show that men have far more difficulty in adjusting to a second marriage than women.

14. FALSE. The University of Oregon studies show that the female begins to talk at an earlier age and continues to be superior in verbal skills.

15. FALSE. Women not only have a greater capacity for happiness, but they also have a greater capacity for UNhappiness than do men.

Scoring:
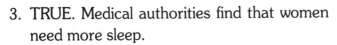

10 or better	Superior understanding of the opposite sex, very mature.
8 or better	Above average understanding of the opposite sex.
5 or better	Average understanding of the opposite sex.
Below 5	Immature, need more understanding of the opposite sex.

After your students have completed the preceding test and discussed their answers, they are ready to turn their papers over and take this test.

How Can I Tell If I'm Really in Love?

1. Did this happen all of a sudden?   YES   NO

2. Would you be very jealous and upset if someone else made a serious play for the object of your affections?   YES   NO

3. When you aren't together, do you find yourself mooning around, unable to do much but think about the other person?   YES   NO

4. Are you more in love when you are together than when you are apart?   YES   NO

5. Do you honestly feel that the object of your affections is just about the most perfect person in the world?   YES   NO

6. Are you, on the whole, pretty unhappy at home?   YES   NO

7. Do you know how your boyfriend/girlfriend feels about money and children?
   YES   NO

8. When you are with your loved one, are you anxious to appear your best in every way?   YES   NO

9. In addition to common interests, do you find you have common miseries with your loved one? Do you have the same complaints about your homes, parents, school, etc.?   YES   NO

10. Suppose your beloved has gone on a long trip and has written you some beautiful, affectionate letters. Would you share these with someone else?   YES   NO

Answers: (By Dr. David R. Mace, Executive Director American Association of Marriage Counselors)

1. NO. Real love does not happen all of a sudden. Each of us develops an "ideal" image in our mind of a desirable mate. When we meet someone who corresponds to the characteristics of our ideal, then we are immediately attracted to them. Love can develop, but it takes time.

2. NO. Jealousy is not a sign of true love. Some jealousy is normal between two people who deeply care about each other, but jealousy is really possessiveness, not love. People who suffer from acute jealousy usually have a sense of insecurity. They need love so badly they cannot bear the thought of losing it; strong jealousy may result from a relationship in which there is no love at all!

3. NO. Real love is directed toward the welfare and happiness of the other person. Assuming the other person is in no personal danger, one should be able to work and study without constantly worrying about the other. If you become absorbed in your own misery at being separated from your loved one, then you are in love with love, not another person.

4. NO. Love does not diminish when one is away from the loved one. If your feeling is more intense just when you are with the object of your affections, chances are that you are simply being dazzled by his or her charm and the excitement of it all. If doubts emerge when you are separated, then indications are that it's superficial.

5. NO. Love is not blind to the beloved's faults. In fact, the real thing is present when you know all your loved one's faults and shortcomings, yet you care deeply nonetheless.

6. NO. An unhappy home can trick you into thinking you are in love. The young person who is constantly battling with his/her parents may leap at the first person who offers an avenue of escape. He/She is not in love, but just wants out!

7. YES. Two of the most important elements of marriage are money and children. People who are really serious about each other must take time to discuss these issues. If the couple hasn't even bothered to talk about these things, chances are their romance isn't very serious.

8. NO. Love does not make lovers feel ill at ease. You should feel completely comfortable and relaxed with your loved one. You should know that your lover loves you for what you are, not because you are constantly trying to impress him/her in manner or appearance.

9. NO. Being companions in misery is not the same as being in love. It is easy to get mixed up in your thinking and falsely identify with a fellow sufferer with whom you want to unite against an unfriendly background.

10. NO. Love is a private bond between two people. It is not likely you love someone whom you would bare intimate details of your relationship to others.

Scoring:
>   10 points for each no, zero for each yes, (except question #7, which scores 10 points for a yes).
>
> | 70 or more | Looks like the real thing! |
> | 50 or 60 | Maybe yes, maybe no, too early to tell |
> | 40 or less | Not yet! |

DOES IT HURT?

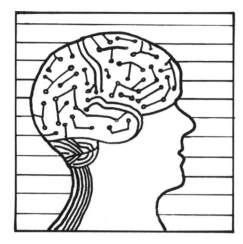

No matter how healthy you may be right at this moment, someday you will become sick. Maybe you still have bad memories about the last time you were sick, thinking about how uncomfortable it was and how much pain you suffered. You might even have been sick enough to go to a hospital and have an operation. When you were lying there in bed, you may have thought: "Why do I have to be sick? Why is there so much pain?"

The body has a very special signal system to warn us when there is something wrong. It is a network of nerves. If you were to take all the nerves in your body, both on the inside and outside, and stretch them end to end, they would extend almost a hundred miles.

This warning system tells us when something is wrong. When we sense the warning very clearly as pain, it is the body's message to the brain to tell us that something needs to be taken care of immediately. But the tragic thing is that many people suffer pain and sickness needlessly, perhaps because of ignorance or maybe willfully. We do so knowing that eating the wrong things may lead to heart trouble or illnesses, that too much starch and sugar make us prone to other diseases, that the excessive use of alcohol makes the body ready for all sorts of discomforts and sicknesses.

Others suffer solely by neglect and delay. George Washington caught a very bad cold one day. His wife urged him to do something about it, but he was too busy. The cold became worse, finally turning into pneumonia, and he died.

Another great President, Theodore Roosevelt, had a very bad toothache, but he had a lot of appointments and he didn't have time to go to the dentist to get it fixed. The tooth became abscessed; that is, it became infected internally when it should have been pulled. Theodore Roosevelt died as a result.

A famous athlete playing tennis one day developed a very bad blister on his foot and it also became infected. The big, strong althlete died from the infection.

So pain sometimes comes to us because of our own folly—because we follow the wrong diet, eat the wrong foods, or we simply just neglect and don't heed the body's warning signal that something is wrong.

If you have any constant pain that comes back regularly from day to day, don't ignore that danger signal. Do something about it; see your doctor right away, and don't be foolish enough to put off little things that need to be done until it is too late. Pain in any form is the body speaking to you saying, "I need repair; I need attention; take care of me immediately."

Activity

To the teacher:

Have your students take a sheet of notebook paper and fold it down the middle vertically. Have them turn it so only the right side is up and write the following:

1. The name of your worst illness.
2. The names of the class, school, clubs, or organizations you belong to.
3. Names of your father, mother, brothers and sisters.
4. Something you would like to accomplish this year.
5. Something you have done which you are proud of.
6. Names of several friends.
7. A hobby you are interested in.
8. Something you would like to do.
9. Name of the church you attend.

Have them turn the folded sheet over to the left side and write the following:

1. _____ died today of _____.
   (student's name)

2. He was a member of _____.

3. He is survived by _____.

4. At the time of his death he was working on _____.

5. He will be remembered for _____.

6. He will be mourned by _____.

7. While he was alive, he was interested in _____.

8. He always wanted to, but never got to _____.

9. Funeral services will be held at _____.

The students can now open up the sheets and read how their obituaries might read if they were to die today.

69

HABITS, THE GOOD AND BAD OF IT

"A habit is a cable; we weave a thread of it every day, and at last we cannot break it."

We are all creatures of habit, but what is a habit? A habit is the tendency to act automatically without carefully thinking about what you are doing. Whenever you do something, the action leaves a kind of an electric track in the gray matter of your brain. Each time you do that same act over and over, it becomes easier to do because there is a tendency for the nerve currents in the brain to follow the same pathway. Eventually you can do the act, such as walking, without even thinking about it. It becomes automatic.

Just think of how terrible it would be if you had to get up every morning and learn how to walk all over again, or how to eat, or how to carry out all the daily tasks; even talking must be learned. If we did not have habits to carry out our daily tasks, we would never get much of anything else done.

How do we learn a new habit, like learning how to play the guitar? You do the same thing over and over, repeating it regularly without fail, till you can do it without thinking about it. How does the tennis player perfect a good serve? By practice!

We have lots of good habits that permit us to carry out our daily routine quickly and efficiently. There are new habits that all of us would like to gain, like learning how to play a musical instrument or being especially skillful at some sport.

We also have **bad habits** that we would like very much to be rid of, like tobacco, or alcohol, or maybe bad language that marks us as not being very courteous to others.

How do you break a habit? The way you break a habit is just the opposite from the way the habit was formed. If you make up your mind that you want to learn a good habit, like playing a musical instrument, you first make a resolution. You determine you are going to learn how to do that skill. If you give up along the way, chances are that you will never gain the skill.

If you want to break a bad habit, you have to do the same thing; make a resolution that you wish to stop and not let the habit happen, not even once. This will not be easy for you. If you have been accustomed to behaving in a particular manner for a long time, it is natural for you to continue doing so. So you must make up your mind that you will not permit yourself to fall back into your old ways no matter what.

A good way is to keep a record on a calendar where you mark off each day that you have been successful. At the end of the week you can check your score. Maybe it's three to seven, maybe it's two to seven, maybe it's a shutout. At the end of the month you can look at the score you achieved for the month and make up your mind that you are going to beat your bad habit with a complete shutout early in the next month.

Here are a few suggestions that may help you with your habits.

First: Don't fool yourself. It's easy to make comments like: "Oh, that's just my way. After all, nobody's perfect." Excuses are just aiding your habit to continue and diminishing your willpower to stop.

Second: Approach your target with a rifle, not a shotgun. Take on part of your habit at a time, not all at once. Shoot down part of it before you take aim on the next part.

Third: Be realistic. Your habit won't be over in a short time; it may take months. Don't give up if you have a few failures along the way; it's long term resolve for freedom that counts.

Finally: Start today. Now is the best time thus far in your life because you've been thinking about it, and you know you have a plan which will succeed.

Ask your friends to help you by encouraging your efforts and by talking with you about how you are going to beat your bad habit. But the real victory will lie with you. Whether you are trying to perfect a good habit or whether you are trying to break a bad one, you are the one that profits the most or loses in the end.

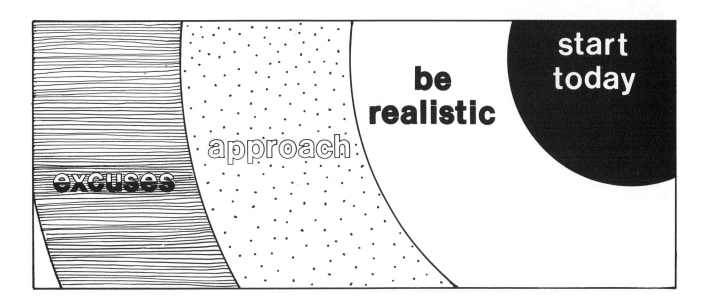

Activity

To the teacher:

Make a ditto sheet of the following list of activities (Part 1). Have students indicate habits they feel they would like to break. Space has been added for students to add their own items to each list. For Part 2 make another ditto, or put on the board for them to copy, a calendar beginning from today's date and going through to the same date next month.

Part 1

Habits I Would Acquire

1. Write letters regularly . . . . .____
2. Be prompt for appointments . . . . .____
3. Do my homework regularly . . . . .____
4. Make new friends . . . . .____
5. Be careful with my diet . . . . .____
6. Play the guitar . . . . .____
7. Exercise regularly . . . . .____
8. Be courteous to others . . . . .____
9. Use correct English . . . . .____
10. Practice a new sport. . . . . .____
11. _____ . . . . .____
12. _____ . . . . .____
13. _____ . . . . .____

Habits I Would Break

1. Exaggerating . . . . .____
2. Procrastinating . . . . .____
3. Being extravagant . . . . .____
4. Using profanity . . . . .____
5. Biting my nails . . . . .____
6. Using alcohol . . . . .____
7. Using tobacco or pot . . . . .____
8. Drinking too much coffee . . . . .____
9. Too much TV . . . . .____
10. Overeating . . . . .____
11. _____ . . . . .____
12. _____ . . . . .____
13. _____ . . . . .____

(Have students now select the one most important item
from each list before distributing the ditto for Part 2.)

Part 2

(Ditto this part on a separate piece of paper to make it resemble a document.)

I, _____, do hereby affirm from this date,

_____, I will:

a. Acquire the habit of _____.

b. Give up the habit of _____.

_____

(signed)

In order to accomplish this, I am going to:

1. Make a calendar for the next month showing success and failure. I will place the calendar where I can see it every morning and mark it every night.

2. Tell my family and friends about my resolution and ask them to help me and encourage my success.

3. Stop kidding myself that I can't do it.

4. Bring my calendar to school next month and discuss my record.

Give your students the choice of returning next month with their calendars. DO NOT require every student to do so, only those you can encourage to participate. Set a fixed date one month hence to discuss their habits score sheet. The teacher should make one for herself, mark it and bring it a month later.

73

BRAVERY BEHIND THE BOOKCASE

Have you ever kept a diary? A bright young girl in Holland received for her 13th birthday a beautiful leather bound book with a clasp to close its gilt-edged pages. Her name was Anne Frank. She made up her mind that, from that moment on, she would write in the book only the most secret things in her life.

One day shortly thereafter, the clack of wooden shoes on the street in front of her house was suddenly changed to the measured tread of Nazi German soldiers as they swept through her country.

Then the Franks received word that the Nazis were looking for Anne's 16-year-old sister. Since the Franks were Jews, it was clear what would happen to Margo and eventually to all the Franks—they would be slipped away to concentration camps to be starved or gassed to death. Papa Frank acted immediately. Anne tells us in her diary of how the family gathered together a few treasured belongings and took refuge in secret rooms in the rear of his office building. A large bookcase guarded the secret entrance to their hideaway. As the Nazi search for Jews became more intense, another family joined them with a teenage son, Peter, and then a dentist came, also.

In a cramped space shielded only by a large bookcase, these eight people lived for years, knowing that to step out into the street would result in certain death. It was not easy. In such close quarters there was bound to be quarreling and bickering. Anne's being the youngest made it especially difficult for her, yet her diary tells us of the little joys, trivial problems, and how she gradually finds herself falling in love with Peter, whom she has first thought to be quite boring.

One day, the unthinkable happened. While searching the house, the Nazi security officer pushed the bookcase aside discovering the secret staircase. The Franks were dragged out and shipped off to certain death in the Nazi death factories. Bravely, Anne faced her fate, although she had committed no crime, done no wrong except to be born into her Jewish family. Although surrounded by the horrors of violence and death, she remained cheerful and sure. Only two months before the Nazis were to surrender, and after years of terror and imprisonment, Anne contracted fever and died in a prison camp. Only her father survived the war.

Her diary documents a continuing positive attitude in spite of all her harrowing circumstances and privations. She never expressed hatred or malice to anyone, even to her Nazi tormentors.

She remains as an example to all of us that, no matter how savage our circumstances, we can face life with a light heart and a clear head.

Activity

To the teacher:

Have your students fold a piece of notebook paper vertically down the middle. On the left-hand side of the paper, write the answers to the following questions:

1. If a close friend of someone in your family had only two months to live, how would you treat him?

2. Should you tell him all the facts of his situation or not?

3. Should his family, friends, acquaintances know all about it?

Now have your students turn the paper over and on the right-hand side of the paper write the answers to these questions:

1. If you were told you had only two months to live, how would you want to be treated?

2. Would you want to know all the facts about your situation?

3. Would you want your family, friends and acquaintances to know all about it?

Now open up the sheet of paper and compare answers. Discuss with your students the differences and similarities of their answers.

Questions for discussion:

1. Can you remember your first personal encounter with death? Was it family? Friends? Public figure? Animal?

2. Do you believe there is life after death?

3. If it were possible to go someplace and look up in a book your date of death, would you do it? Why?

13 DEATH

4. Have you ever thought about suicide?

5. What medical efforts should be made to keep seriously ill people alive?

6. How important are funerals for the survivors?

Complete the following:

I, _____, being of sound

mind, do this date, _____, make my last

Will and Testament. I hereby bequeath the following:

1. _____

2. _____

3. _____

(List at least three things.)

_____

(signed)

A BRIGHT IDEA

The Story of Thomas A. Edison

A scientist has been defined as a person who is able to solve a difficult puzzle of nature but who is also able to recognize a question unrecognized by others. The young six-year-old Thomas Edison fell into the latter category as he stood looking at his father's barn.

"I wonder what would happen if I set fire to it," he said to himself. Tom had learned the way to find out about things was to experiment with them; the barn was no exception.

The results of his experiment were twofold: the barn burned to the ground, and Tom's britches burned for some time after Dad Edison put him over his knee for a hard spanking. Fortunately, this early experience didn't discourage young Tom to give up his experiments or his curiosity, for by the time he reached maturity he was probably (and still is) the most famous inventor on Earth.

Edison's brightest idea was electric lighting. But we also owe him thanks for originating record players, motion pictures and the alternating current generator. He was popularly called the Wizard of Menlo Park, after the name of the laboratory in which he worked; but Edison knew that he was no wizard. His main magic was hard work. "Genius is one percent inspiration and ninety-nine percent perspiration," he told reporters. He knew that a good idea took a lot of persistence and long, hard hours of effort to make it work. Edison had the idea that by electricity, he could produce a lamp to light the homes of the world inexpensively. "Impossible!" said the well-known scientists. "It cannot be done; the laws of electricity won't permit it."

Edison discovered that when some scientists found a problem difficult, they simply gave up on it. He also found another strange thing that many other original people have discovered: noncreative people distrust and even dislike the creative individual, although they may be quick to praise him when he solves a problem.

The inventor searched to find out all he could on the subject of electricity and lighting, an odyssey that was to fill the pages of two hundred notebooks. His idea was to pass an electric current through a wire, heating it white hot; it would then give off a bright light. The problem was to find a substance which would not burn up, even in the vacuum

created inside a glass bulb. He tried literally thousands of different substances, even including human hair, but they all burned up after a short time. To his amazement, an unlikely candidate turned out to work quite well; thin strips of bamboo glowed in the vacuum tube and were tough enough to last long enough to be practical. But it was a long way from the laboratory to a comfortably lighted home. Special generators had to be invented. Switches, control gauges, and even a new meter had to be invented to measure the amount of electricity used by each home. All of this took years; yet Edison worked on day and night, sleeping a few hours on the floor of his laboratory and then back to his workbench to struggle with the next problem. By now he had a team of scientists working with him, but he could not delegate the problems to them since he was the only one who really understood the problems in the first place. Not only did he undertake the scientific problems, but he also had to solve the political problems of having the streets of New York dug up and buildings and houses wired for his new invention.

Finally, the great day came. All the world waited as Thomas Alva Edison threw the switch. Great cheers broke the air as the city of New York sparkled with electric lights. Soon the whole world would follow. Scientists immediately hailed him as the greatest inventor who ever lived; but he did not stop there. Ahead lay the motion picture camera, the motion picture projector and many other inventions that make our lives easier and happier in this difficult world.

He proved a bright idea will soon die unless a lot of hard work is devoted to bring it into reality. Edison might have said, "If you want to leave footprints in the sands of time, you had better wear work boots."

Activity

To the teacher:

Ditto the puzzles and distribute them to your students with the following instructions:

1. This is not a test and will not affect your classwork in any way.

2. Here are some interesting puzzles which have several possible answers. Try to give the *best* answer.

3. Do not be afraid to be persistent with a puzzle you cannot solve quickly, but do not spend more than ten minutes on any one. On the other hand, do not rush through them.

Put the following on the chalkboard:

Here is an example.

What are the fewest number of cuts you can divide a cake into eight equal pieces? Show a drawing of your answer. Give a reason for your answer.

My answer is:

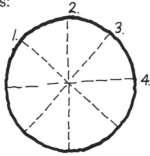 (a good answer)

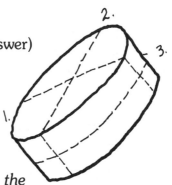 (a better answer)

Reason:

I decided that cutting the cake in the middle horizontally was better because it only required three cuts; however, there is the problem that it may be difficult to make this cut exactly in the middle.

Part 1: After the students have been given about thirty minutes on the puzzles, discuss each one on the board, having various members of the class suggest possible solutions. **All** puzzles are possible; however, do not propose a "right" answer since that will prohibit the use of this exercise with other classes in the future.

Part 2: Now divide your class into teams of four or five, depending upon the class size, and distribute the second set of puzzles to the teams for a group solution. After thirty minutes, have each team report on its solution and then have the class rate the best solution to each puzzle.

ARE YOU CREATIVE?

Part 1:

1. Which is worth more: a piggy bank filled with £ 5 gold pieces or the same piggy bank filled with £ 10 gold pieces? Tell why you decided on your answer.

2. Shown is a Japanese line picture of a martini glass with an olive in it. What is the least number of lines to move to get the olive outside the glass, without moving the olive?

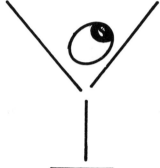

3. There are 10 glasses in a row: the first 5 are full, the second 5 are empty. What is the least number of glasses to move in order to move them alternately full, empty, full, empty, etc.? Please show a drawing of your answer.

4. Imagine you are drinking a soda. How would you leave in the bottle an amount that was equal to half the volume, using the least amount of equipment? If possible, show how; if not, tell why.

5. A clock takes 5 seconds to strike 6 o'clock. How many seconds will it take to strike 12 o'clock? Tell why you decided on your answer.

ARE YOU CREATIVE?

(Team solutions)

Part 2:

1. What is the **most** number of pieces, equal or unequal, you can cut a pancake into, using just four cuts? Show a drawing of your answer. Explain.

2. It is easy enough to put 11 pennies into three cups so that each cup holds an odd number (3,7,1), but is it possible to put 10 single pennies into three cups so that there is an odd number in each cup? If so, show how. If not, tell why.

3. The Queen keeps her diamonds in a box with a sliding lid on its top. To stop thieves, she has a live, deadly snake inside the box. One day a slave was left alone in the room for only a few minutes. He managed to steal several of the gems without taking the snake out of the box or touching or influencing the snake in any way. And he wore nothing to protect his hands. The theft took only a few seconds. When the slave left the room, the box and the snake were in exactly the same condition as before, except for the loss of several diamonds. How could the slave have done it, using little or no extra equipment? If possible, tell how. If not possible, tell why.

4. A boy and a girl ran a 100-meter race. The girl crossed the finish line when the boy had gone only 95 meters. When they raced a second time, the girl decided to make the race more even, so she handicapped herself by starting 5 meters behind the starting line. If they both ran at the same speed as before, who won the race and why?

5.
```
F A T H E R
H E R M A N
L O U I S A
I S A B E L
```
It is easy to divide these names horizontally with three lines into four names, but can you divide the four names by only two lines? If possible, show how. If not, tell why.

Questions for discussion:

1. Did you give up when a puzzle seemed difficult, even though all of these puzzles have solutions?

2. What kind of attitudes do you think are helpful to the creative solution of a problem?

3. Was the team solution to a problem easier or more difficult than trying to solve it by yourself?

4. Is it easier to "think out" a puzzle with a paper and pencil or in your mind only?

5. Was there someone on the team who seemed to be more creative, or did everyone contribute ideas?

6. Do you think it is possible to "learn" how to be a better problem solver, or are you just born with the ability to solve problems?

Solutions:

Part 1:

1. SAME. Gold is valued by weight; the same volume will have the same weight.

2. NONE. Just tilt your head or the paper.

3. POUR #2 into #7, and #4 into #9. Better solution; none. Pump #2 into #7 and #4 into #9.

4. TILT bottle until liquid is just at edge of mouth and top of bottom.

5. 10 SECONDS. If 5 seconds for 6, then double for 12 or 10 seconds.

Part 2:

1. INFINITE NUMBER. Roll up the pancake. Cut into spiral.

2. YES. Put one cup **inside** another; then put 3 in second cup and 7 in the other.

3. TURN box upside down. Slowly slide lid until diamonds drop out.

4. GIRL wins again. At 95 meters, they are both even. Since the girl runs faster, she will be slightly ahead after the last 5 meters.

5.

F	A	T	H	E	R
H	E	R	M	A	N
L	O	U	I	S	A
I	S	A	B	E	L

MY BEST FOOT FORWARD

Have you ever said to yourself at one time or another, "I can't do anything. I wish I had some talent." Of course, that's not correct. You do have talent! Everyone has *some* talent. The problem is you need to honestly appraise yourself, discover what your talents are and develop them. That calls for some hard self-appraisal and then some hard work and persistence.

How do you discover your talent? How do you know what you're skilled in? How do you know what you can do better than anything else?

The first important thing for you to do is to look for hidden urges that are within you. Maybe you read a poem or a book and said to yourself, "Oh, I wish I could write like that." Or perhaps you've watched an athletic contest and thought, "Oh, I wish I could play the way those players are playing." Or maybe you listened to some thrilling music and thought, "I wish I was a musician." Or maybe you had a teacher and thought to yourself, "Oh, I wish I could teach like that." All of these things may be a clue as to the talent that is within you. Psychologists tell us that until we find out what we want to do most in life, then we will never really be happy.

If you talk to a lot of older people and ask them, "Are you doing what you would like to do in life, I mean, really what you would like to do?" many of them will tell, with a sense of disappointment and frustration, that they wish they were doing something else; that they wish that they were living someplace else. Oh, it may be true they may have been successful; that is, they have made a good living in what they were doing, but they have missed the real joy of doing something they are particularly talented in.

Galileo's parents wanted him to become a physician; he preferred mathematics, instead. Joshua Reynolds, the famous Renaissance painter, had his parents come to him one day and say, "Why do you waste your time scribbling pictures all the time?" Today, he is one of the most famous artists who ever lived. The father of Handel, the great composer, wanted him to become a lawyer. Handel had to learn music by himself, snatching a moment here and there whenever he could sit down and play the organ. Goldsmith, the great author, was a complete failure in formal learning, yet he had a great desire to write.

Do you have a yearning for something that you would like to do more than anything else? It doesn't have to be something special, like being an artist or a great composer or even a great novelist. It's just something that you enjoy doing and you never seem to get tired of it. You'll never know what your hidden talent is unless you explore some of your hidden urges now while it's not too late.

Don't be like so many adults, who find themselves working all day long, every day, at a task they dislike. Develop your talents, because you already have a head start over everyone else. You are interested in it!

Activity

To the teacher:

Ask your students to take a sheet of paper and write down a list of twenty things they enjoy doing very much.

To encourage your students, you might suggest to them that the things they list can be big things or they can be little things that are particularly important to them. Perhaps they could start with the seasons of the year or the different days of the week. They should not list routine things like eating and sleeping.

After they have listed as many activities as they can think of (there may be more or less than twenty), then have them rank the first five things they enjoy doing the most in order of preference.

Now divide the class into teams of two, each student paired with a partner. If there is an odd student, the teacher should team up with the extra student. First one partner tells the other the advantages, pleasures, benefits or satisfactions he gets from each of the five activities, but NOT in the order of preference. The listener then guesses what order of preference the speaker prefers to do each activity and makes a prediction as to what life occupation the speaker would do well at. After the speaker has informed the listener how close he came, the roles are then reversed. The speaker becomes the listener and vice versa.

After both team members have had a chance to share their favorite activities, the teacher should ask the students to turn their papers over and on the back complete the following sentences:

A. I realize that I _____

B. I was surprised that I _____

C. I was pleased that I _____

These statements can be negative as well as positive, such as "I realize that I am not sure about what things I really like to do." These statements can be shared with the class, or the teacher can select one person and interview him about his activities.

T.L.C.
or
Teresa's Loving Care

After she was awarded the 1980 Nobel Peace Prize, Mother Teresa was asked by reporters how she was called to her lifework in India. She replied, "It is not how you are called, but how you respond that counts."

Agnes Famoraneck had come a long way from the peaceful village in Yugoslavia where she was born with her brother and sister before World War I. Like a modern legendary saint, the citation read, "She has poured out her life in the service of others and has undoubtedly been instrumental in saving the lives of thousands."

Agnes would never have thought of herself in these terms, although she attended church regularly and loved to listen to the stories of the nuns and priests who cared for the sick and starving. She soon made up her mind that she would dedicate her life to serving others as a nun. At age 18, after she had finished her schooling, she decided to go to Ireland for training, since they would accept her at this young age for her early training. Following her service as a novice, she asked to be sent to a major city in India where she might best meet the needs of the outcasts of humanity. She was sent to India's largest city, Calcutta. There, with much dedication and prayer, she completed a course of study to become a nun.

Sister Teresa, as she was now called, gathered teen-age girls around her as a teacher, showing them the same love and care she had received as a young girl back in her own home. But she soon realized the beautiful gardens and campus of the school were like an island in a great sea of tragedy. Outside on the crowded streets of Calcutta lurked misery, disease and horror. Homeless, naked, starving children wandered the streets, abandoned by their parents. Among the dead and dying in the gutters were those half alive, half dead from the dread disease of leprosy. Thousands simply had no home or shelter to protect them from the weather. In the morning the dead were carried off to be burned.

Although she had become headmistress of her school, Mother Teresa could no longer bear to retreat from the great human tragedy outside the walls of her school. She resigned from her school responsibilities and enrolled in a short course in nursing. She then found a vacant lot to open her own school for the homeless.

On the first day, five, dirty, ragged children appeared. They knew nothing of learning or even how to use indoor plumbing facilities. Mother Teresa cared for them as though they were her own. Soon hundreds of children began to pour in. This meant she must

solic funds and other people to help her. Many of her former students now joined her as teachers, and the news of her efforts drew support of money, books, medicines, furniture, and used clothing.

Just when it began to appear there was no end to the avalanche of homeless children, a group of young nuns came to help her. Together they formed a separate order called the Missionaries of Charity.

Encouraged with this support, Mother Teresa now opened a haven for the sick and dying in an old vacant church. The church had not been built as a hospital, but Mother Teresa and her coworkers demonstrated that the most important aspect of a hospital is T.L.C. or "tender, loving care," not fancy equipment or prompt efficiency. The lame, the lost, and the lepers came flooding in. Tiny newborn babies left in the gutters or rubbish cans to die were cared for. Many were so sick that they soon died, but many were, and are, nursed carefully back to life.

Following her Nobel Prize, Mother Teresa's homes were jammed with newspaper reporters and television cameras. A very well-known TV commentator remarked, "The most striking characteristic of these nuns who carry on this back-breaking, fearfully endless job is their attitude of complete peace and joy, and secondly, the loving tenderness they shower on each of the unfortunates within their care. No doubt much of this must come from Mother Teresa, herself."

The Nobel Peace Prize is usually awarded to famous statesmen who have affected the political destinies of nations. Rarely is it given to someone who has personally saved the lives of thousands and has established an organization to continue doing so for many generations to come, yet most agree that this recognition was probably one of the best ever given.

Activity

To the teacher:

Have your students fold a piece of writing paper in half and on the left side ask them to write realistic descriptions of how they think their lifestyle will be fifteen years from now.

Ask them to include what they think their life occupations will be with an approximate income, the kind of home, neighborhood, and what state they will be living in. If married, describe their spouse, how many children, if any, and their approximate ages. Have them tell how much they think they will owe on their house and cars and furniture. They should tell what community activities and hobbies they will be participating in and what they think it will be like to live in America by then.

Having completed this, they should now use the other side of their papers to describe the same thing; only this time there should be NO limitation on trying to be realistic. Let them dream of whatever they feel would be the most realistic situation they can imagine for themselves.

Questions:

1. What is the main difference between these two predictions of your future?

2. Is the limitation in the first prediction imposed upon you or created by you? Are you limiting your own view of yourself?

3. In your view of the future, did you include any obligation to serve the community or to take any responsibility for shaping your own future?

4. Do you think the things which are important to Americans today will be the same fifteen years from now?

5. Do you think the possession of money and things makes people happy?

THE GREAT WIZARD AND THE KING
Legend of Magic

The   "I cannot go another step." The great wizard dropped to his knees, then fell back on the forest grass.

"But Master," spoke his apprentice softly. "I heard the sound of a festive gathering. We cannot be but a short distance from the king's castle."

They both paused, listening for a moment. Sure enough, across the glade came the sounds of music and the short happy cries of laughter. The apprentice held out his hand and the white-haired, gaunt figure struggled to his feet and moved in the direction of the sound.

As they entered the crowded dining hall, the king instantly beckoned the wizard to join him at the High Table. "My, you look exhausted," said the king as the wizard settled into a great chair, his apprentice standing dutifully behind him.

"And you never have looked better, Your Majesty. All that is said about you is still true. You are indeed the handsomest man in the land, although I have not seen you for many years."

"Who are all these people, and what is the celebration about?"

"Oh, these are just politicians, nobles, rich merchants, and many plain curiosity seekers who have come to see if I really am as handsome as everyone says. We are not celebrating anything special. I do this almost every night. It gives me great pleasure."

"Such a happy gathering! I can see you have no need of a wizard."

"I am pleased you came as a guest, but if I ever need you, I will let you know."

Several years later, the wizard was busy in his mountain cave when there came a loud knock on the door. The apprentice came running back from the entrance.

"It's the king! The king himself is at the door!"

True enough, the king himself stood in the doorway. Quickly the wizard welcomed him into the cozy, but cluttered inner recesses of his laboratory. They sat down in front of the fire, its flickering light revealing the king's face. His once smooth skin had now turned yellow, the eyes appeared sunken and dark with wrinkles at the corners. His once sharp chin had become double, and his tall frame was bent with a puffed-out belly.

"How may I help you, Your Majesty?" queried the wizard.

"I am a sad man, for my mirror tells me that I am no longer the handsomest man in the land. I have consulted the physicians for pills, medicines, and potions, but they only make me feel worse! I have paid great sums of money for special creams, mineral waters, and mud packs. I have even had a mystical spell cast upon me, but nothing helps. Then I remembered you. Surely you can use your powers where everyone else has failed."

The wizard looked into the fire for many minutes, then he turned to the king.

"Your mirrors have lied to you. You must find the magic mirror that will alone tell you the truth. But I warn you; it will not be easy. The mirror is hidden deep within the forests of these mountains, and it can only be found alone and on foot, early in the morning at sunup. When you find it, you will see yourself handsome again."

"Thank you, great wizard. I will start early on the morrow."

At daybreak on the next day, the king set out searching the hills. Day after day, he tramped through the forest. No longer could he hold great feasts with rich wine and late hours. Instead, his days were filled with vigorous exercise and fresh mountain air.

Months went by until one day there again was a great knock on the wizard's door. The king did not wait but burst in upon the wizard.

"I have found it! It is true! I am handsome again. The magic mirror tells me the truth!" He held up a broken bit of mirror. The apprentice hardly recognized him. Gone were the yellow skin and double chin. Restored again was the erect, trim, muscular stature of a true king.

The wizard removed his pointed hat and carefully looked the king straight in the eye. "I cannot lie to you. I hid that mirror you have. There is nothing magic about it, but it does tell you the truth. The truth is that vanity and rich living robbed you of your fair appearance, and hard exercise and healthy hours have restored it. Your gift of beauty must be worked at just like any other gift, or it will soon be lost."

As the king walked slowly back down the mountain, he made up his mind that he would not forget the fine lesson the wizard had shown him.

Activity

To the teacher:

Make a ditto sheet of the following twenty questions, and ask your students to answer yes, no, or maybe.

I AM SOMEONE WHO:

1. is likely to have four or more children.

2. will probably take up smoking.

3. will never visit a foreign country.

4. will always read the comics no matter how old I am.

5. will marry someone who is rich.

6. will run for public office.

7. is likely to grow fat.

8. will not permit my hair to get gray naturally.

9. will change my religion.

10. is sure to move away from my home community.

11. is apt to get into trouble with the law.

12. may develop a drinking problem.

13. is likely to smoke pot.

14. dislikes my mother.

15. will make a poor parent.

16. drives much too fast.

17. will never have much money.

18. probably will not go to college.

19. isn't fussy about the kinds of food I eat.

20. is not much interested in exercise.

After they have answered the questions, ask them to select those questions to which they gave definite yes or no answers. Underneath the twenty questions, they are to write at least five more statements expressing their own personal goals for the future. Example: I am a person who _____ (expressing their own personal goals for the future).

From the twenty questions with definite yes or no answers and from their own statements, they are now to write a paragraph describing themselves for an imaginary computer which will match them up with someone else with similar tastes and attitudes for a blind date (also imaginary).

HE HAD STARS IN HIS EYES

"Space is a new ocean and this nation must sail upon it."

President John F. Kennedy

From the moment primitive man first gazed upward through the eons of time to this very day, people have dreamed of flying off this earth to explore the distant stars. Until this generation such thoughts were just idle dreams, but for one young farm boy growing up in the rural island of Hawaii, these dreams were to become a reality.

Don't think it was easy. Astronauts are very special people, chosen only after a long, exhaustive selection process. It began one day when Ellison Onizuka's school principal came to his home in Kona, Hawaii, to inform his parents that their son wanted to fly into space as an aerospace engineer.

His mother was shocked. How could they afford to send him to the university? But his father told Ellison, "Son, we have no property or money to give you, but we can provide for your education, and in America, maybe that is more important than property . . . ."

With a modest scholarship, Ellison entered the University of Colorado as an engineering candidate. Back home in Kona, his father drove a taxi and worked in the coffee fields, while his mother tended their small store to make ends meet.

To match their efforts, Ellison excelled at the university, winning top scholarship awards plus the Air Force's "Outstanding Achievement Award" as an ROTC officer. Upon graduation he was assigned as a Test Flight Engineer for the Air Force. A short time later he completed the Test Pilot Training School and became a flying aerospace engineer.

When the opportunity came to apply to NASA as an astronaut, Ellison was quick to submit his papers although he knew only thirty-five would be selected out of 8000 applicants, and out of the thirty-five trainees, only a handful would fly into space. Long years of training, education, and discipline made the difference, and Ellison was jubilant at his selection for astronaut training. His first flight was of the STS, one of many to follow.

At 8:23 a.m. on January 28, 1986, Ellison Onizuka joined six other star voyagers on the launch pad aboard the space shuttle *Challenger*. The last public glimpse of Ellison was a twinkling, boyish smile and that winning gesture of "thumbs up." Because of the record cold weather the countdown was delayed until 11:38. At T-minus 10 seconds, the loudspeaker blared, "We have main engine start." *Challenger* thrust upward. Amid the roar Mission Control ordered, "*Challenger* go at throttle up!" Commander Scobee replied with the last words from *Challenger*, "Roger, go at throttle up."

The *Challenger* flew off into the mystery of the future.

Ellison Onizuka's dream has become our responsibility. He proved that every person could fulfill his potential by looking beyond his limitations. In a talk given at age 14 to his 4-H club, Ellison said, "The term *American* ends with two words: *I can*. I am proud to be an American." The rest of us are also proud that you were an American, Ellison.

Activity

To the teacher:

Divide your class into groups of eight or less. Draw the shades, light a candle in your hand and turn off the lights. Have students sit in circles, each circle with a lighted candle in the middle.

Tell them to imagine that they are all trapped in a damaged space station orbiting the earth. The station has been struck by a random meteorite, destroying the electrical system and soon the remaining oxygen will be lost. The emergency shuttle must be launched immediately before all electricity and oxygen are gone, but it will only hold four people.

Each person will take the candle and tell why he should be included with those who escape. Each person should tell what good things he has to give to the world, what his plans are for life, how he could benefit others, how much others back on earth may need him, or whatever reasons he feels are important to be a survivor.

The teacher should keep the mood serious by going first and telling his own story, perhaps resigning in the end as the responsibility of a leader. After the teacher has done so, he should pass the candle to a verbal student who will speak next and so set the pattern around the circle.

After everyone has spoken, take a secret ballot vote to determine which four will go. The teacher may or may not reveal who has been selected, depending on the group.

Turn on the lights. Have the class now respond to these questions either verbally or in writing and present their answers orally.

1. Why did you have a hard time telling the good things about yourself?

2. Do you think that the person who said nothing or very little should be left behind?

3. Have you ever thought of your life plans before? Have you considered how you might be important to others?

4. Do you think that people who are burdens to society should be cared for at taxpayers expense? How about prisoners?

5. Would you be willing to donate your heart or some vital part of you to keep some important scientist or government person alive? A movie star? A popular musician? (Look for contradictions from those who said very little.)

6. If someone close to you told you he was going to commit suicide, what would you say?

7. Did you think those who were selected to escape really had something to contribute to the world or were they chosen simply on the basis of popularity?

DON'T, DON'T, DON'T

"Man, if there's anything that gives me a pain, it's being ordered around all the time."

"Don't drive too fast."

"Don't stay out too late."

"Don't waste your time; get your homework done."

"Don't make such a mess; clean up your room."

"Don't do this and don't do that. Sometimes, I could just scream."

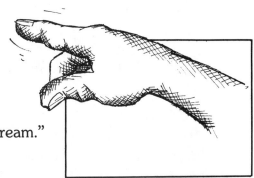

This sounds like a situation which no young person should be in, but many kids feel they get orders so thick and fast they could just go berserk. After awhile they think that rules ought to be for the new players on the team and that clipped wings are for the birds.

Worst of all, many adults follow up the orders with moldy phrases like, "It's for your own good" or "When I was your age . . . ."

There must be some reason why everybody's uptight about all these things they want young people to do and not do. Right. There is a reason. It's because order is important. It's important in your home, in your school, and mighty important in sports. What kind of a game would you be able to play if there were no rules? How well do you think the team would play if they didn't take orders from the coach?

What would our community be like if we didn't have traffic lights or other rules to keep people from stealing and hurting each other? Without order our world would be a mess. Your help is needed to keep your home and school going right. The smart young person is the one who learns to listen and pay attention.

Socrates, the Greek philosopher, once said: "I hope I never get too old to listen to advice from a wise person."

So you are smart if you pay careful attention to the words of those you respect, like your teachers, your parents, your coach. They are trying to help you avoid the pits and lumps in the road of life, since they have already been down the road.

It's true that Mom and Dad should not always be on your back bugging you, but remember when you take orders, someday you will be in a position to give them.

One of these days you'll be given the keys to your own car and your own home. These keys will open the door to your own life, and then it will be your turn to give the orders.

Activity

To the teacher:

Begin this activity with a discussion on how your class (or school, neighborhood, community, nation) could be made a better place. When students suggest the elimination of homework, remind them that this would also require the elimination of grades and credit; but discuss how the homework schedule could be improved. After they have decided on several factors for improvement, have them make up several rules to implement the changes.

Put the rules on the board and take a vote on the rules they would like to put into effect. Keep a careful record of those who vote "no" and those who do not vote. Now have the students decide what the punishment should be for infraction, decide how it should be monitored and who should enforce it. Have them live with the rule for at least a week or more. If it becomes obvious that the rule is a problem, remind them that the rule can be changed at any time.

Questions for discussion:

1. Should all students obey the rule even though some voted against it or did not vote at all?
2. Did you participate in the discussion before the rule was made? Did you participate in the vote when the rule was decided upon?
3. Did you feel the rule and its punishment was just?
4. Did you participate in the discussion and vote when deciding how the rule should be enforced?
5. Is it easier to let someone else make up the rules or to make up your own?

At the end of the discussion, the teacher should summarize how rules (laws) are decided upon in our society and how they are enforced, how they can be changed, and what happens if everyone does not participate in their formulation.

94

WHAT MAKES THE TEAM EFFECTIVE
The Story of George Washington

American farmers and frontiersmen were quick to defend their rights when the British sent highly trained professional soldiers against them during the Revolutionary War. Most Americans had never fired a gun in anger, yet they were expert marksmen, using the famous Kentucky long rifle as a weapon. It was not unusual for American riflemen to be able to knock out the eye of a squirrel at fifty yards, and yet they were disciplined and accustomed to leading highly independent lives on their homesteads, many of which they had hacked out of the wilderness with their own two hands with determined spirit. What they needed to face the experienced British troops was an outstanding leader who not only understood the early American character, but also the sophisticated enemy that these patriots had volunteered to fight. Such a man was George Washington.

Hard pressed at the beginning of the war, the Continental Army moved as quickly as it could to avoid direct confrontation with the larger, well-equipped British force. Carefully studying the map one day, General Washington noticed a stream ahead blocking the passage of his supply wagons and artillery. He called to one of his lieutenants to send a detail of men ahead to fell several trees across it so that by the time the main body reached the stream, they could cross more easily. Late in the afternoon, General Washington rode ahead to check on the bridge construction. As he approached the tree felling site, he noted that very little had been accomplished, and that if things proceeded at their present rate, the army would be hopelessly bogged down when it arrived at the river.

The corporal in charge was giving many orders, telling his men to do this and do that, and the soldiers responded the best they could; however, there were just not enough of them to get the job done very fast. General Washington could see that they would never be finished in time, working at their present rate.

Flinging his heavy riding cape around him to cover his Commander-in-Chief's uniform, the general rode forward to the little group of toiling soldiers.

"Hello there. How are you getting along, Corporal?"

"Well, sir, there just aren't enough men to get this job done."

"You mean you need a lot of help to finish the job?"

"Yes, sir, if we are to get these trees cut and across the river before sundown."

"If you are behind, why don't you pitch in and give a helping hand yourself?"

"What? After all, sir, I'm a corporal. It wouldn't be fitting or proper for me to roll up my sleeves and get my uniform soiled working with ordinary soldiers. I have to maintain my position as a military supervisor."

"Of course," said the mounted officer. With that he slid down off of his horse. He carefully tethered it to a nearby tree, slipped off his cape and jacket and set to work with the soldiers felling and clearing and carrying the large trees to the river. He showed himself to be as fit and able as the youngest man among them. In a short time, the task was well-accomplished.

Mounting his horse, he turned to say, "Corporal, if you have another difficult assignment and you need more men, be sure to send for the Commander-in-Chief, and I will be sure that you get some help."

As he rode off, his cape furled over his shoulder revealing the gold epaulettes of the Commander-in-Chief.

"Good heavens!" exclaimed the corporal. "That was General Washington himself!" He sank down on the ground. "And I let him work while I sat around and did nothing."

Activity

To the teacher:

Have the class team up into teams of two. If there is one without a partner, have him join a team of two. After the teams have been formed, then indicate the student whose birthday is nearest to April 1 to be team captain.

Make a ditto sheet or put the following topics on the board:

1. Describe how your life would be different if there were no TV.

2. Tell how you will be different than your parents are when you grow up to be a parent.

3. Describe the kind of person you DO NOT wish to be when you grow up.

4. List at least five things that would make this school (class) better than it is.

5. If you could change one thing in your life, what would it be and how would it change your life?

The team captain now selects one of these topics, or another one of his own choosing, and must write at least a two-paragraph response WITH THE ASSISTANCE OF HIS TEAM MEMBER. The team member should give as much help as possible, up to and including actually writing the paper; however, the teacher should emphasize that ONLY the team captain's name will appear on the paper and that only he will be graded on its content. Set a definite time limit for the completion of the paper.

After all the papers are turned in, then announce that roles are now to be reversed; the captains become the team members, and the team members are now to act as the captains. The writing exercise is repeated. The teacher must carefully note who is on each team during the writing period, since the papers will have only the captain's name on them. At the conclusion, the teacher announces that the two grades will be averaged for an overall grade for each participant.

Questions for class discussion:

1. Did you prefer to be a captain or team member? Why?

2. When you were captain, did your team member give you some real help? Did you give leadership to the effort?

3. Could you have written a better paper alone? Why?

4. When you were captain, do you think you got a better or worse grade than your team member when he was captain?

5. When you were a team member, did the captain seek your help, or did he ignore it?

THE FOWL FOWLER
(Anglo-Saxon folktale)

What would you say if I asked you what a fowler is? No, he is not someone put out of a basketball or hockey game. A fowler is one who captures birds by throwing a net over them, much the same as a fisherman casts a gill net to catch fish. Many medieval fowlers learned to whistle birdcalls so that they could imitate a distressed bird in the woods. This would attract other birds to the scene who were then promptly captured and carried off to the village market.

The favorite bird for eating, and thus in most demand, was the quail. Quails were captured in such great numbers that there became a very real possibility of extinction.

One day the chief quail gathered all the other quails together in the forest to consider the problem.

"This has got to stop!" he said. "If we don't do something, our kind will forever disappear from the earth."

"There's nothing we can do," replied a lesser quail. "When that net drops over us, we are trapped. All the struggling and flying in our power cannot get us out of the net."

"You're right! In fact, that's just the problem. We are so intent upon trying to escape, we flutter and struggle madly, just becoming more and more enmeshed in the net."

"So what do you suggest we do?" they queried.

They all listened carefully as their leader explained exactly what they were going to do the next time that nasty net tumbled around them.

The next day one of the most expert fowlers came into the woods looking for his prey. Stealthily he crept up to the covey of quails who appeared to be peacefully picking seeds from the forest floor. With a deft motion of his arm, he cast the net over the entire group of birds.

"All right, everyone," said the chief quail. "Don't panic. All together now, when I give the word. Here we go! Fly! Fly!" With those words, each bird calmly picked up the net in his beak and began flapping his wings. The whole covey gently rose off the ground carrying the net with them as they went. The fowler stood there dumbfounded as he watched his expensive net being carried off into the blue sky.

The quails were jubilant! "We did it!"

"They'll never catch us again!"

"We not only got away, but we took his net, too. He'll never use that to capture birds again!"

So saying, they dropped the net at the top of a tall tree.

All went well for awhile, but as they repeated this successful performance, they became more and more confident and boastful. Finally, they started quarreling among themselves about petty things such as who carried the heaviest part of the net or who flew the highest, until some birds refused to even speak to other birds. Their quarreling grew so loud that some of the other animals thought they were no longer quails but magpies.

Sure enough, their loud scolding attracted a fowler on the hunt with his brand-new net. No one noticed him since they were so busy disputing with each other. Zip! The net fell over them, trapping most of the birds beneath its deadly drape.

Immediately, their leader gave the usual command to lift off together, but instead of working together, they fluttered and flew every direction, becoming more and more entangled. They were all captured.

As the fowler carried them off to market, their leader sadly said, "You see, when we worked together and helped each other, we were safe. When we got proud and boastful, we were easily captured."

All the birds agreed, but by then it was too late.

Activity

To the teacher:

Divide your class into groups of five or six, depending on your class size. Make a ditto of the following information and give it to each group.

The Decision

Imagine that the time is twenty years from now. The world has just suffered a nuclear holocaust and is now so radioactive that it is no longer habitable. A shuttle rocket is on the pad, ready to blast off and take your committee plus FOUR other people to a space station from which a long-range mission will be launched to find another liveable planet.

Waiting outside are ten other people who are available to go with you. Your committee must decide by majority vote which FOUR of the ten will accompany you. Very little is known of these other people and there is no time for further investigation, although it is likely that from this group will come the beginnings of a new human race on some other planet.

You have fifteen minutes to decide from the following list which four (or less) will escape with you.

1. A white male rock singer, talented musician, age 23, known heroin addict.

2. A white college professor of history, age 72.

3. A black Olympic athlete, age 26, ex-convict for rape and robbery.

4. A white prostitute, age 32, now "retired."

5. A white clergyman, age 54, speaks four languages.

6. A white female (his wife), nurse, age 47. These two refuse to be separated.

7. An Oriental second-year male medical student, age 22, a known homosexual.

8. A white male lawyer, former state governor, resigned because of misuse of government funds, age 55.

9. His young, crippled daughter, age 9.

10. An Oriental female schoolteacher in mathematics, age 27, divorced because of refusal to have children.

As each committee deliberates, the teacher should give time warnings of ten minutes, five minutes and one minute.

The committees can then share their selections and give the reasons why. The teacher might keep a tally to see which of the ten received the most bids to escape.

The teacher should now tell the class to disregard their selections and think more carefully on HOW these selections were made by answering the following questions:

Questions: (to be written)

1. Was everyone listened to in your group, or were some members ignored?

2. Were you persuaded to change your mind and to "go along with the group," even though you didn't agree?

3. Is it OK to "go along" with the group to achieve harmony so a decision can be reached, even though you disagree?

4. In your group discussion, was there any one person who assumed the lead? Who? Was that leadership positive (unselfish) or negative (selfish)?

5. Was there any consideration that one of the committee be eliminated in order that someone else on the list could go?

6. How do you think your selections showed what you think is important in life?

THE SWORD OF DAMOCLES

(Ancient Greek legend)

Dionysius was the king of the ancient Greek city of Syracuse. In the days of the Greeks, it was much easier than it is nowadays for a common man to get to know the king. Such a common man was Damocles, who became very friendly with his monarch Dionysius. When they were talking one day together, Damocles said, "You must be the most contented man in the world with the wealth and luxury you enjoy."

"Ah," said Dionysius, "you haven't yet been to one of my royal feasts, have you?"

"Well, no, I haven't."

"You must come tomorrow night. I will have you sit in the most honored place and meet some of the most distinguished people in the kingdom."

"Oh, I would be most delighted to attend."

The next day, Damocles purchased a set of new fine clothes and that night presented himself to the guard at the palace gate.

"Oh, yes," said the guard. "So you are Damocles. The king told me about you. Please come this way." He led him inside and down a long passageway to a great dining hall filled with people. When the king saw Damocles he beckoned for him to come over and be seated on his right hand beside him.

Damocles was overwhelmed by the beautiful statues, the rich tapestries and the priceless silver on the tables. "I really don't deserve to be here," he said.

"Oh, yes, I think you do," said Dionysius. And he leaned back in his great royal chair with a curious smile on his face.

Damocles looked about the room filled with many prominent people, all luxuriously dressed, chatting with one another.

Then he glanced up above him and horror filled his heart. Suspended over his head was a razor-sharp, double-edged sword held only by a single strand of horse hair. It gently swayed as the servants moved across the hall bearing great platters of food and goblets of fine wine.

His first impulse was to jump out of the way, but that would surely offend the king who had seated him in the place of honor. People spoke to him, but Damocles did not hear them; instead, his thoughts were on the sudden death suspended over his head. The plates of food came and went, but Damocles did not taste any of it although he ate some of each thing that Dionysius offered him. He hoped that this dreadful meal would end quickly.

Finally, Dionysius rose. "My friends, it is time for us to move into the courtyard to listen to the royal musicians."

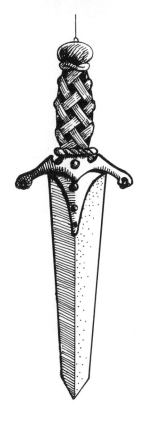

Suppressing an impulse to jump out of his chair and run, Damocles rose slowly out of his chair away from the deadly dagger suspended over his head.

"My dear Damocles," said Dionysius putting his arm around him, "I'm very proud of you for suffering through the feast the way you did. But you must understand that the life of a king is not all ease and luxury but filled also with fear and apprehension. My sons plot to kill me, my ministers lie to me and I am the target of assassins. I could resign and give it all up much the same as you could have gotten up from your chair and left us, but you were brave and chose to stay. With privilege comes great responsibility. You have faced it only one night, but I must face it every day. Consider yourself lucky that you are Damocles and not Dionysius."

Damocles came many times to visit Dionysius, but he never forgot that first night.

Activity

To the teacher:

Have your students pair up in teams of two, preferably a boy and a girl. If the students are shy, have the boys count off in even numbers (don't explain why); then have the girls count off in even numbers. Pair up the consecutive numbers (1 & 2, 3 & 4, 5 & 6, etc.). If there is an odd student, then the teacher should pair up with the extra student.

Now have the teams face each other for three minutes and carefully study each other by observing each other in detail, trying to remember each little detail about the other person. Partners should then turn their backs on each other. They now have three minutes to change five details about themselves (reverse wristwatch, unbutton one button, comb hair differently, etc.). Once rearranged, they then turn back and face each other again. They now have three minutes to write down the five details they observe that have taken place.

The teacher should keep score. Have the champion detectives face each other, changing as many details as possible. Give a prize for the winner (a mock detective badge, a candy bar, etc.).

Questions for discussion:

1. What is the most noticeable thing about another person? Compare boy answers with girl answers. Why did you choose this aspect as being most noticeable?

2. Without looking, how many people in this class are wearing glasses?

3. Does a person's appearance tell something about personality? What?

4. Can you tell something about a person's character by the little details of his/her appearance?

5. Should a person be judged by appearance? Are people sometimes "labeled" by their appearance?

Recommended reading: *The Return of Sherlock Holmes* by Sir Arthur Conan Doyle

FREEDOM FOR ONE ONLY

(A true story of Toulon's Prison)

Activity

To the teacher:

Make a ditto of the following true story and work sheets for your class to use with it. If you read the story to them, try to dramatize the various parts of the prisoners to help them empathize with each one.

After the story has been read, distribute the work sheets. Part I should be answered by teams of four or five who give a joint report. They may be interviewed by the class members or the teacher concerning the reasons for their conclusions. Parts II, III and IV should be answered individually and then discussed in class.

Resist a consensus on Part IV, since this leads to the idea that there is a "right" answer.

(The Prince released the confessed thief with the
admonition, "What a pity for an evil man to be
confined with all these innocent men. I cannot allow
you to remain in their company another day.")

A French Prince visited Toulon, a city well-known for its terrible penitentiary. In honor of its royal guest, the Warden offered to release a single prisoner, whomever the Prince might designate.

The Prince said to the Warden, "Have the prisoners elect the three most deserving prisoners; they will know who should go free. Then send them to me. I will decide which one should be released."

The next day three men came to the Prince, each telling his story of imprisonment. The first man said:

"I was in love with a rich merchant's daughter. He did not wish me to marry her since my family was poor. One day when I came to visit, he met me at the door saying, 'Here is a ruby ring. You may keep it, but with it goes my request that you see my daughter no more. If you decide not to, I will send you a diamond cane to go with it.'

"Just then his daughter appeared before I could say anything. The next day officers came to search my room, finding the ring. They arrested me for stealing. On the witness stand the merchant said I had stolen a family treasure. I am innocent. My beloved waits for me, while I am imprisoned for the rest of my life for a crime I did not commit."

The Warden added he had been a model prisoner and the merchant had later been arrested for perjury on another case. His daughter came to visit regularly and had often proclaimed his innocence to the Warden.

The second prisoner had this to say:

"I deserve to be here. I have cheated and stolen from my employer who trusted me.

My trial was fair and my sentence was just. I have begged my employer for forgiveness, but I cannot repay the money I took from him. At least I can repay my debt to society. Thank you for considering to release me, but I am sure there are others who deserve freedom more than I do."

The Warden said there was no doubt he was a thief, yet his employer had asked for leniency at his trial, but the judge chose to make an example of him for other possible thieves.

The last man had this to say:

"I am a Black from North Africa. I am the oldest of a family of eight children. To help my family, I worked very late at night. One evening, on my way home, three men fell upon me, struck me on the head, tied my hand and foot, and carried me down to their ship.

"When we got out to sea, I was released and forced to work as a deck hand. When the ship reached Toulon, I tried to escape, but the mate siezed me. In the fight that followed, I am sure he meant to kill me since I had seen him kill other men. During the fight, he struck his head, fell overboard and drowned.

"The Captain said that I had murdered him so I have been here ever since and will be here until I die unless you release me."

The Warden said his family from North Africa had been to visit him and that he was a gentle, mild person whom all the other prisoners liked.

Which one would you have released? Before you make up your mind, look carefully at the next "fun game work sheet."

106

Carefully fill out the following work sheet.

We know as a matter of history which one the Prince released (second prisoner), but he may have made a wrong choice. Before we decide, we should consider some important factors which might influence our conclusion.

I. What do you think the importance of a prison is:

A. A place where society gets revenge against wrongdoers?

B. A place where bad people are punished so they won't do the same thing again?

C. A place where criminals are isolated away from society so they won't harm people anymore?

D. An institution that attempts to change the criminal so he can fit into society again?

E. A place that is so unpleasant, people will think carefully before they commit a crime?

II. On the basis of your ideas of what a prison is, do you think the Prince should have released one of the prisoners because he felt:

A. He should show mercy to the most deserving prisoner?

B. He should attempt to accomplish justice?

C. He should choose a prisoner who is ready to return to society?

III. How could the Prince decide which of the prisoners was telling the truth?

A. Is this really important?

B. Do you think most prisoners claim they are innocent?

C. Could the Prince rely upon the information given to him by the Warden?

IV. I would have released _____.

V. On the basis of your decision, describe the effect upon the following:

A. The rich merchant whose ring the court adjudged stolen.

B. The daughter who was waiting for her lover to be released.

C. The family of the black man who waits for his release from a foreign prison.

D. The community and the judge who convicted the confessed thief.

GENERAL DEAN'S ADVICE

"Honor, Service, and Courage" is the motto of the Honolulu Police Department. Honor is certainly important in our society because it involves having a keen sense of what is right and what is wrong.

Our country was founded by men of great honor. Ethan Allen, who made history with his "Green Mountain Boys" fighting during the Revolutionary War, was once brought to court because of an unpaid debt.

His lawyer, who appeared at the bar for Ethan Allen, thought that perhaps the best defense was to claim that the note Ethan Allen had signed was a fraud and a fake.

Whereupon Ethan Allen cried in anger, "Sir, I did not hire you to come here and lie for me. I wish you only to tell the truth. The note that I signed is genuine, and the signature is mine. All I wish is for the court to grant me sufficient time to make payment of my just debt." Ethan Allen was a man of honor.

In 1888, William Coleman's firm finally went bankrupt, owing well over $2 million. Mr. Coleman legally could have ignored all of the debt that he owed, but he didn't. He went back to work, working twice as hard and he made an entirely new start. Within four years he had paid off all of the debt that he owed plus the interest for the time that he had kept the people's money while he was unable to pay them back. Mr. Coleman was an honorable man.

During the Revolutionary War, when the thirteen colonies were fighting for freedom, the British came to General Joseph Reed, who was a very influential member of Congress. They offered him $50,000, in addition to a very high office in England, if he would help bring about a reunion of Great Britain and the rebelling thirteen colonies. General Joseph Reed replied, "I am not worth purchasing, but such as I am, not even the King of England is rich enough to buy me."

Probably of all the many honorable men who helped found America, the most outstanding was George Washington. It's not true that George Washington chopped down his father's cherry tree or that he threw a dollar across the Potomac River. However, there are many legends about George Washington which are true. When George Washington was notified of his election as President of the United States, he said, "Be the voyage long or short, although I may be deserted by all men, I will never be deserted by integrity, by firmness, by honor. They shall never forsake me." An honorable man is as good or better than his word.

General Dean, who was the commander of the American forces in South Korea, was captured by accident by the enemy. He was kept in solitary confinement and locked in a small, dark closet, where he was forced to sit cross-legged on his knees for days and days. General Dean was finally given the opportunity to write a single letter home, in which he wrote this advice to his son. "Do not seek wealth and riches my son, but honor and integrity. These are the most important things." General Dean, like George Washington, was an honorable man.

Activity

To the teacher:

Tell your class members they will need a partner to play this very fascinating game. After the class has paired up, divide them into groups of four teams. If some are left over, use them as timekeepers, judges, and recorders.

Hand out the ditto sheet of the "High Score Wins, Pay Off Schedule and Tally Sheet." Give each pair a red and blue colored marker, poker chips, or pieces of colored paper.

Go over the ditto sheet with them so they understand how to play the game. At a signal, they are to simultaneously display the color chip of their choice, which will determine their score, depending on the pattern of colors displayed by their entire team.

Keep careful time, announcing the bonus rounds, and monitor their scoring to keep them honest. At the conclusion of the ten rounds, they may wish to play the game again now that they have "caught on" how to play it. After they have played several games, tell them to total up their group score to determine the winner. It is not the individual pairs' scores that count, but rather the GROUP score that determines the winner.

They can now turn their score sheets over and answer the following questions in writing:

1. Rate the teams in your group from "Most Honorable" to "Least Honorable."

2. Would your group have done better if everyone had been honorable?

3. Was there displayed a feeling of distrust in your group? Why? Did it have anything to do with honor?

4. Why do you think nations are unable to live together peacefully in the world community?

5. Did you try to play this game in an honorable way or not?

6. Is winning always the most important thing?

109

HIGH SCORE WINS

Pay Off Schedule and Tally Sheet

How to play the game:

This game is played in ten rounds. Some rounds will score more than others. You and your partner will choose a color, either red or blue. The points scored will depend upon the pattern of choice displayed by everyone in the group according to the following table:

Strategy:

You and your partner will be given time to confer before each round to help you jointly decide which color to display. Before rounds 5, 8, and 10, you will have the opportunity to confer with other members in your group.

4 Blue	All win 1 point
3 Blue 1 Red	Lose 1 point each Win 3 points each
2 Blue 2 Red	Lose 2 points each Win 2 points each
1 Blue 3 Red	Lose 3 points each Win 1 point each
4 Red	All lose 1 point each

Round	Time	Confer With	Choice	Points Won	Points Lost	
1	1 min.	partner				
2	30 sec.	partner				
3	30 sec.	partner				
4	30 sec.	partner				
5	2 min. 30 sec.	group partner				bonus double
6	30 sec.	partner				
7	30 sec.	partner				
8	3 min. 30 sec.	group partner				bonus triple
9	30 sec.	partner				
10	3 min. 30 sec.	group partner				bonus five times

THE FARMER, HIS SON AND HIS DONKEY

(A legend of Aesop)

A farmer came in from the field one day. "Wife," he said. "Today I am going to the market to sell our donkey so we will have seed to plant next year. I am taking our son with me to help carry the grain when we return."

The three of them soon started off down the road with the father leading the donkey, the boy following along behind. A short distance down the road they came upon two milkmaids who began giggling and laughing.

"What's so funny?" asked the farmer.

"You have such a strong, able donkey, and yet you let your poor son walk behind in a cloud of dust," they replied.

With that the farmer immediately reached down and put his son up on the donkey's back, and they proceeded on until they came to a crossroad. There they met an old man.

"Which way to town, old man?" asked the farmer.

"That way," he said, pointing his finger. "But it's a long way to walk, especially for a poor father. Young man, why don't you have some consideration and let your father ride? After all, you are young and healthy."

The boy looked at his father and then slid down from the donkey's back. His father mounted the animal, and they started down the road which led to the town market. Shortly, they came to a stream.

"How deep is the water in the middle?" asked the father of a woman who was washing her clothes along the bank.

"Oh, it's much too deep for the lad. You'd better take him up with you when you cross."

The father motioned the boy up behind him and they slowly made their way across. They had not gone very far along the road on the other side when they came upon a friar walking along the way. When he saw them he shook his head disapprovingly.

"Don't you know that it is a sin to be cruel to dumb animals? How terrible that you two healthy people should overload that poor dumb beast! Why don't you both get off and carry him?"

The father dismounted. "We do not wish to sin, Father." After making the animal lie down, he tied the feet together and slipped a long pole between the legs. With great effort he and the boy lifted the pole to their shoulders and started down the road to the bridge which entered the town.

The heavy burden of the donkey became even more back-breaking as they ascended the bridge. The farmer swayed a little, then fell to his knees. As he did so, the donkey tumbled over into the river to drown in the swift current.

They turned to walk back home and the farmer reflected bitterly on their journey. "Why did I ever listen to what other people said? Why didn't I do what I knew was best in the first place? Now we've lost our donkey, and we shall have no seed to plant for our crop next spring—all because we tried to please others instead of doing what I knew was right."

Activity

To the teacher:

Divide your class into teams of five or six depending on your class size. Make a ditto sheet of the following and distribute it to each team:

What Really Counts

I. a. Of all the religions and philosophies of man, there is now, or there will be someday, one that describes the ultimate truth.

b. It is impossible for mortal man to ever know the ultimate truth.

II. a. An honest, thoughtful person can know that what he believes is right.

b. It is possible for the beliefs of an honest, thoughtful person to be wrong.

III. a. As man develops through the centuries, he is getting better and better.

b. Human nature is the same as it has always been for thousands of years.

IV. a. In any given situation, there is at least one right course of action.

b. There are always many courses of action to follow in any given situation, the choice being a matter of personal preference.

V. a. A person should give considerable thought to his "afterlife."

b. A person should live his life to its fullest and not spend too much time worrying about his "afterlife."

VI. a. The reason we have religions is because man has inner fears and worries.

b. The reason all men have some kind of a religion is because all men have a deep sense of the supernatural.

112

Have each team make a report on Section I, giving the reasons why they selected either a or b. The teacher or the class could interview them on the reasons for their stance. Now have them do the same for Sections II and III. After they have reported their positions on these issues, tell them they may shift to any other group of their choice.

Have the newly formed groups report on Section IV, then shift again, report on Section V, then shift, report on Section VI.

In most cases, the class will divide itself into two or more distinct groups. Some groups will show a unity of opinion; some groups will simply be a circle of friends.

Questions for discussion:

1. Did you move to another team? Why?

2. Did you generally agree with the team you ended up with?

3. Were you influenced in answering Sections I, II, III, by how the others in your group felt, or did you stick to your original viewpoint?

4. Which is more important: to stay with a group you disagree with and try to influence them toward your point of view or change to a group with a common viewpoint?

5. How did you feel toward those who disagreed with you? Were you receptive or did you reject their views?

EYAM

(From the walls of Eyam Parish Church)

Eyam is famous for an event which took place three hundred years ago and which has stirred the hearts of men ever since. This was the visitation on the village by the Great Plague from London, at the end of August 1665. The story unfolds of how a parcel of cloth was brought by carrier from London and set down at the door of the local tailor, a man called George Viccars, who lived at a cottage still standing just west of the churchyard. Unfortunately, the cloth had become infected with the Plague germs before being dispatched, and the tailor soon became the Plague's first victim in Eyam. At this stage it would have been easy for the remainder of the inhabitants to seek safety in flight. Had

they done so, they might have been responsible for spreading the Plague over a large part of the North of England, and it is to their eternal glory that acting under the inspired leadership of two men, William Mompesson, rector of Eyam, and Thomas Stanley, who had been his immediate predecessor, the inhabitants voluntarily cut themselves off from contact with the outside world, so that the pestilence should not be spread elsewhere. It meant death for many of them, for during the fifteen months that the Plague did its dread work, 260 persons perished out of a presumed total population of 350. In the fields in and around Eyam you can see mute memorials to that sad time in the form of tombstones erected over victims who were buried near the places where they died, for example, the Riley graves, where members of the Hancock family lie buried, and the Lydgate graves in the village.

Activity

To the teacher:

1. Have the students make up a rule they think would make their school (classroom) a better place to learn. Have several students read their rules or tell them to the group.

2. Choose one of the rules (controversial, if possible) and have the students vote on rules until they decide upon one rule.

Questions for discussion:

a. Should all students obey the rule even though some voted against it or did not vote at all?

b. Did you participate in the decision and the discussion before the vote was taken?

c. Is it easier to follow someone else's rules or to make up your own?

d. Do you always follow the rules?

e. What do you think should be done with those who do not follow the rule the classroom has decided upon?

3. Have the students discuss the punishment for those who break the rule they have made up. Try to bring them to a group decision by vote, as to what the punishment should be.

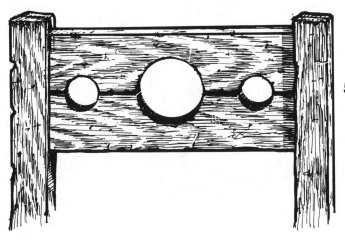

4. After the group has decided on the punishment for an infraction, try to live with the rule for a few days, but remind the class that the rule can be changed at any time.

5. Summarize with them how rules (laws) are decided upon in our society, how they are enforced, and how they are changed if they don't work. What happens if everyone does not participate in their formulation?

FAMOUS HANDS
The Story of Albrect Durer

Long ago in a small village in Germany there lived two young brothers, Albrect and Franz. They were part of a very large family who all worked hard every day so there would be enough to eat. Everyone in the village agreed that both young men had an extraordinary artistic talent. Their drawings and sketches of village life showed that they possessed great artistic ability and a keen insight into the character of the individuals they portrayed. There were no art schools in those days; instead it was customary for a young person with talent to go off to some large city where he would study and learn from one of the great masters of the time.

But for Albrect and Franz, this presented an insurmountable problem. How could they go off and leave their large family without their support and where would the money come from to pay for their lessons from a famous master?

"Ah! I have the answer," said Franz. "You go to study painting and I will stay and earn the money to support you. Then when you are finished, you can work and pay for my training. That way we both can become artists."

It sounded like a good idea to Albrect, so he agreed to do his very best to learn all he could while Franz worked hard to pay all the bills. The best paying occupation available to Franz was the back-breaking labor of working in a smithy: heating, pounding and forging hot metals. Yet Franz worked longer and harder than anyone else so he could earn the wages of two.

Albrect also studied hard and won great praise for his work, both from his master painters who guided his technique and from his fellow artists. Eventually, he finished his studies and joyfully returned home.

"I'm finished, Franz! The Master says he can teach me no more. It's up to you now. I have made arrangements for you to enroll immediately."

Franz did not look at his brother; instead his eyes dropped to the floor. Then he finally looked up at Albrect and raised his hands before him. They were the broken, gnarled, calloused hands of a smithy, useless to an artist.

"I can no longer even hold a brush, Albrect. I'm afraid I can never be an artist now."

Albrect was grief stricken. With tears in his eyes he grasped his brother's broken fingers in his own delicate hands saying, "There is only one way in which I can even begin to repay you. I shall draw a picture that will speak to men's hearts—a picture of these hands of sacrifice and love."

Today, hundreds of years later, the picture of the praying hands is known the world over. Albrect Durer became one of the world's greatest painters, but he never could have done so without the love of his brother, Franz.

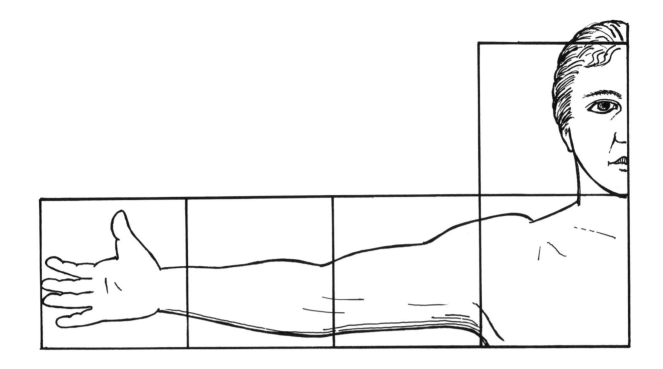

Activity

To the teacher:

Divide the class into two teams. Try to match size and physical ability of opposing team members, since this will be a contest of stamina and muscular skill.

Have the teams gather around, select a team name and a team captain. Each team should then determine its own cheer and give it loudly to the rest of the class. Now that they have generated some team spirit, you are ready to explain to them the contest.

Tell them they are about to play a fun game requiring silence and teamwork. The two teams should line up, one behind the other, with the team captains last. No talking from this point on.

At a signal from the teacher, they are to raise their arms so they are extended horizontally, not above or below their shoulders.

The first person to lower his arms causes that team to lose the game. Team members may assist each other by fingertips ONLY, and of course, NO TALKING.

Questions for discussion:

1. What kept you from lowering your arms when it began to "hurt"?

2. Did you feel you were a good team member or a poor one? Why?

3. Win or lose, were you satisfied with the performance of your team?

4. Does teamwork require just cooperation or an effort?

5. How did your team captain help his team or not help them perform?

KING KATZYA

(Adapted from the Talmud)

During his lifetime he was called Alexander the Great because he had conquered most of the world. But today he is known as Alexander of Macedon, after the Greek province where he began as a young student of Aristotle.

Although he ruled a vast empire, Alexander always valued the possibility of learning from a wise man. So when he was told there was a very wise king named Katzya, he started off immediately to visit him.

Upon his arrival, he was greeted and welcomed by Katzya. "Our little kingdom is flattered to be host to the ruler of such a great empire."

"I am come to learn how wisely you rule your country and learn the laws of your land," said Alexander.

"Ah, then you must come tomorrow to the Judgement Hall and you may see our laws in action."

The next morning Alexander was escorted to a place of honor beside King Katzya as he sat in court to settle the disputes brought before him. The bailiff entered with two men.

"Your Majesty, these two were found fighting in the marketplace. Each one accuses the other of dishonesty."

Katzya beckoned to the first man. "You may speak on your own behalf," he said.

"Your Majesty, I bought from this man a field of land which contained a large scrap heap. I paid him a just sum for it and he gave me title to it. As I cleared the scrap heap, I came upon a bag of gold coins worth a great value. This treasure is now rightfully mine since it was part of the scrap heap that I purchased."

"Not so!" said the other man. "Had we both known of the gold coins, we would have decided on a completely different price. I do not ask for the gold coins, but just my fair share since we both bargained, not knowing they were part of the purchase. Giving me my fair share will cost this man nothing, since he did not know it was there in the first place. Cure this man of his greed, Your Majesty!"

Katzya thought for a moment; then he said to the first man, "Do you have a son?"

"Yes, Sire," the man replied with a puzzled look.

"And you," said the King to the other man. "Is your household blessed with a daughter?"

"Indeed it is," was the reply.

"Then I hereby decree that these two shall marry and the treasure shall belong to them."

"You are truly just, Oh Great King," said the men. And they left, their dispute settled, but Alexander just smiled.

"How would you have handled the case, Alexander?" asked King Katzya.

"It's simple. I would have put them both to death and confiscated the gold."

"You feel gold is more important than justice?"

"Gold is more important than anything," replied Alexander.

That night all gathered in King Katzya's palace for a royal feast. Alexander was delighted to be served his favorite dish, roast pheasant, but when he tried to cut into it his knife struck solid metal. It was gold.

"What are you trying to do to me?" demanded Alexander.

"Ah," smiled Katzya, "I knew you thought gold was more important than anything, even food. But perhaps you have changed your mind. Gold is important but it must not rule us. We must rule it. That is especially true for kings, would you not say?"

"You are truly wise, Katzya. I have learned my lesson."

Before he finished speaking, a delicious real roast pheasant was placed before him, and Alexander joined all the others in a tribute to the wise King Katzya.

120

Activity

To the teacher:

Tell the students the class is going to do a special experiment. Select four to eight volunteers who are willing to pay 25¢ (or less) to take part in the experiment. If there are not enough volunteers for the experiment, tell the class there is a chance to make some money from the experiment.

The class should then gather around in a circle with the volunteers in the middle. The teacher then collects 25¢ from each volunteer.

Explain to the volunteers that at the end of a given time limit (five minutes) the group must decide which one should get ALL of the money. Make it clear that all of the money must go to only one person. No deals or splits after the experiment, or the teacher will keep the money. The teacher should be careful not to appoint any leader, but leave the decision entirely to the group.

Questions for the class after the experiment: (Leave the money out for all to see until after the experiment.)

1. Was there any consideration of who needed the money the most?

2. Do you think justice was done?

3. Did you notice that any one person displayed leadership in solving the situation? Did he display positive (unselfish) or negative (selfish) leadership?

4. Was luck used to solve the problem? If so, why?

5. What money values do you think the members of the group showed in solving the problem?

OLIVER TWIST

by Charles Dickens

The room in which the boys were fed was a large stone hall with a copper at one end, out of which the master, dressed in an apron for the purpose and assisted by one or two women, ladled the gruel at mealtimes. Of this festive composition, each boy had one porringer, and no more—except on occasions of great public rejoicing, when he had two ounces and a quarter of bread besides. The bowls never wanted for washing. The boys polished them with their spoons till they shone again. And when they had performed this operation (which never took very long, the spoons being nearly as large as the bowls), they would sit staring at the copper with such eager eyes, as if they could have devoured the very bricks of which it was composed. A council was held, and lots were cast who should walk up to the master after supper that evening and ask for more. It fell to Oliver Twist.

The evening arrived and the boys took their places. The master, in his cook's uniform, stationed himself at the copper; his pauper assistants arranged themselves behind him. The gruel was served out, and a long grace was said over the short commons. The gruel disappeared and the boys whispered to each other, and winked at Oliver, while his next neighbors nudged him. Child as he was, he was desperate with hunger and reckless with misery. He rose from the table and advancing to the master, basin and spoon in hand, said, somewhat alarmed at his own temerity:

"Please, sir, I want some more."

The master was a fat, healthy man, but he turned very pale. He gazed in stupified astonishment on the small rebel for some seconds, and then clung for support to the copper. The assistants were paralysed with wonder, the boys with fear.

"What!" said the master at length, in a faint voice.

"Please, sir," replied Oliver. "I want some more."

The master aimed a blow at Oliver's head with the ladle, pinioned him in his arms, and shrieked aloud for the beadle. The board were sitting in solemn conclave, when Mr. Bumble rushed into the room in great excitement. And addressing the gentleman in the high chair, said:

"Mr. Limbkins, I beg your pardon, sir! Oliver Twist has asked for more!"

There was a general start. Horror was depicted on every countenance.

"For more!" said Mr. Limbkins. "Compose yourself, Bumble, and answer me distinctly. Do I understand that he asked for more, after he had eaten the supper allotted by the dietary?"

"He did, sir," replied Bumble.

"That boy will be hung," said the gentleman in the white waistcoat. "I know that boy will be hung."

Activity

Demonstrating for a Cause

To the teacher:

Put a list of controversial issues, of which the students have definite opinions, on the chalkboard. Here are some possible suggestions, but solicit as many more from your class as you can.

1. There is too much homework at this school.

2. Marijuana should be legalized.

3. Students should have their own smoking lounge.

4. There should be a student court to punish school rule breakers.

5. McDonald's should take over the cafeteria operation.

6. Students should be able to recommend or disapprove of hiring or firing of teachers.

7. Compulsory education in high school should be eliminated.

8. There is/is not racial prejudice in this community.

9. Lunch periods should be made longer and the school day shorter.

10. There should/should not be a national draft into the armed services.

After the students have added their own suggestions to this list, ask them to select one of these issues they feel strongly about. The teacher should try to promote or select outright one of the topics which the class is clearly divided upon.

Divide the class now into two groups, those for and those against (these need not be equal). Then distribute poster board to each student. Each student should now write his own slogan on his poster board.

Examples for "Marijuana should be legalized."

After each student has made his sign, those in the minority should get up and hold a demonstration by marching around the room. They may chant their slogans, if they wish.

The teacher should remind the students that the U.S. Constitution guarantees freedom of assembly to *peacefully* seek redress of grievances. This obviously precludes violence or infringement on the rights and property of others. Those observing the "demonstrators" should be reminded that just as they expect to be listened to, so should they give the courtesy of their attention to those now demonstrating.

When the minority has finished, the majority may now rise and demonstrate their cause. The teacher should be careful this activity does not become too boisterous. It should be done with fun, but with care.

After the demonstrations, each student should come to the front and explain his slogan and give his opinion on the subject. Again, caution the students to remember their responsibility to listen to the other side of any question.

After a discussion, the class is now ready to vote by secret ballot to decide the issue.

THERE COMES A TIME WHEN WE MUST PAY THE PIPER

The little town of Hamlin was infested with rats. They were everywhere. They were in the baby's bed, they were in the kitchen, they were in the living room, they were in the attics; they overran the city. They fought with the cats. They chased the dogs off the streets.

Yes, people were desperate. Everyone tried to think of some way to get rid of the rats. Lots of people made suggestions, but nobody could come up with an idea that really worked. People were becoming more and more impatient with the mayor and the city council for not taking some kind of public action to rid the town of rats.

One day, there appeared at the mayor's office, a very unusual looking young man. He called himself the Pied Piper. He said he would have no difficulty removing the rats from the city of Hamlin. He told the mayor he would simply play on his beautiful pipe and all the rats would be charmed and follow him outside of the city.

His price for this service was a thousand dollars. The mayor was extremely happy and agreed that he would pay the thousand dollars, if the Pied Piper would indeed rid the city of Hamlin of their rat problem.

So the young man walked out into the street and put his pipe to his lips and began to play the most marvelous, strange tune the people had ever heard. From everywhere came the rats—big ones, little ones, brown ones, black ones, spotted ones. They followed him down the street and down to the river where they tumbled in and were drowned.

As the Pied Piper walked back up to the mayor's office to claim his thousand dollars, the people shook his hand and patted him on his back and greeted him with smiles and congratulations. But when he got to the mayor's office, the mayor said, "No, I'm sorry. Our city treasury is empty, and we cannot pay you." He laughed at him and told him to come back next year.

The Piper said, "If that's the case, I can play my pipe again and in a different tune."

So he stepped out into the street and again put the pipe to his lips. This time from everywhere came the children of the city. Laughing, happy, bright-eyed, they followed him down towards the river. The townspeople watched with horror, too shocked to move, thinking he would lead them into the river also, but he did not. Instead, he stepped aside and led them up to the mountain. There the side opened up and all the children went inside and were swallowed up, never to return. That was the last that the town of Hamlin ever heard of the Piper and all of their children.

Well, that is an interesting fairy tale which many of us have heard, but what it means is that when we make a bargain, we always have to pay our part of the bargain.

Today, in an affluent America, there are lots of things to buy and lots of things we would like to have, but they all have a price. That price must be paid even though we buy the article on credit. In fact, if we buy it on credit, that makes the price even more.

Maybe you've heard of the young man who wanted to go to his school carnival, so he asked his parents if he could have all of his allowance for a whole month ahead. Having collected his allowance, he went to the carnival and spent all his money, but then a week later, he was again begging his parents for more money, since he had already spent it.

Or maybe you've heard of the young lady who wanted to have a brand-new dress to wear on a very special occasion, but was not willing to do the baby-sitting jobs to earn the extra money.

Yes, all of us have many things that we would like to have, but we have to learn in life that everything has its price, and you can't have what you want unless you "pay the Piper."

Activity

To the teacher:

This is a fun activity in which the teacher will have to invest a few dollars.

Announce to the class that you are going to auction off six 50¢ pieces to the highest bidder. Assure them that no credit will be allowed and that only cash deals will be made at the conclusion of each bidding.

Hold up a coin and announce, "I have here a silver 19__ (Kennedy, Silver Eagle, etc.) genuine half dollar, good at McDonald's or any store in America. What am I bid?"

Keep a record on the board of the high bidder and the price each successful bidder pays for the coin. Be sure to have a handful of pennies to make change.

Questions for discussion:

1. Was the bidding faster when the price was higher or lower? Does the price have something to do with the number of buyers?

2. Is the price of an article based on what it is actually worth or what people are willing to pay for it?

3. Did the winning bidder have any advantage over the other bidders?

4. In our free enterprise system, the price of each coin was determined by competitive buyers. In a communist system, all of the money would have been divided equally among the whole class, with a little more going to those with good grades and a little less to those with poor grades. The government (teacher), makes up the loss between the actual value and the amount the whole class is willing to bid. Which system is best? Why?

After you have discussed these questions, split the class in half. Have them sit on opposite sides of the room; do not mention they may cooperate. Repeat the auction with four more 50¢ pieces.

Questions for class discussion:

1. Would there be any advantage of everyone on one side of the room cooperating with each other instead of bidding against each other to get the coins for themselves?

2. Do you think that labor and management compete with each other in our free enterprise system to drive the prices up?

3. In what two industrialized nations in the free world does management and labor cooperate? (West Germany and Japan)

4. In communism the two groups would have decided on a price and divided the money equally. Which do you think is the better way? Why?

PORTRAIT OF A LEADER
The Story of Saladin and Richard I

Horror swept through Christian England. Wandering knights brought word that far off Jerusalem had been captured by the barbaric Saracens. These terrible Mohammedans, led by their cruel King Saladin, had cut the throats of the faithful Christian defenders and had forever forbidden any Christians to enter the Holy City again. The people were incensed. Priests and bishops held massive meetings. Kings and princes gathered together and it was decided that King Richard the Lion-Heart should lead an army of Crusaders to capture Jerusalem. *Crusaders* means "marked with a cross," since every knight in King Richard's force was to wear a cross on his battle dress.

After about three years, the English knights began to return home, but without their king. Had he been killed? Did they capture the Holy City? What of the bloodthirsty King Saladin? When asked these questions, the knights would often just walk away without answering because, instead of accounts of bravery, victory and overcoming a wicked enemy, they had quite a different tale to tell.

First of all, Saladin was not the real name of the Saracen king, but just a nickname given to him by his people meaning "honor of faith," because he had spent his youth studying with great scholars about his religion. He would have remained immersed in his library, but since he came from a family of warriors, he was forced to go to war against the Egyptians. He quickly demonstrated that he was as good a soldier as he was a scholar. Before each battle he spent hours carefully examining all the possible moves of his enemy, much the same as a master chess player. During the fighting, he would ride along the battlefront encouraging his army, but when he came upon a troup in trouble he was quick to ride into the foray, fighting shoulder to shoulder with his men. It wasn't long until he had not only defeated Egypt, but also Syria to the north. That left a narrow strip of land in between, the territory we today call Israel. In those days it was called the Holy Land.

It was ruled by Christians who had captured it about one hundred years before. Although it was supposed to represent all things sacred to the Christians, those who lived there were very cruel and often attacked the Mohammedan community. Saladin ordered his army to sweep in and capture Jerusalem. Terror filled the city as the people remembered the slaughter of Saracens that had followed the victory of the Christians. They need not have feared, however; Saladin killed none of those living there, not one. He permitted those Christians who wished to leave to buy their freedom and ordered all ancient religious buildings to be left untouched.

In time, King Richard arrived in the Holy Land with his great army of Crusaders. He captured the city of Acre and when he did so, he immediately slaughtered over 2000 Saracen prisoners. After another great victory all the Christian princes began quarreling among

themselves over the loot they had captured. There followed a great dispute in which Richard tried to remind them of their religious purpose, but many decided that if they couldn't have what they wanted, they would go home. Off they went, leaving Richard to continue to struggle alone. He did his best, but he soon realized his weakened force was no match for Saladin. Further, he discovered that Saladin was no barbarian. He always kept his word, unlike the Christian princes. One day Richard fell ill and lay burning with fever. Saladin sent his physician with quantities of snow and fresh fruit. The Christian princes wanted to murder them. Richard struggled from his sick bed with sword drawn to defend the servants which Saladin had sent to his aid.

Finally, Richard met with Saladin to make peace. They agreed that the Crusaders could retain control of some of the seaports, and that Christians would be permitted to visit Jerusalem whenever they wished to do so.

Richard started home to England, only to be captured in Austria by one of his Christian comrades-in-arms, who held him for a huge ransom. As Richard languished in a cold, dark dungeon on Christmas Eve, he must have reconsidered the noble cause which had taken him from England, for it would be many months before he would return.

As the truth about what had really happened came back to the people in England, surely they must have begun to wonder who was really the greatest leader, Saladin or Richard the Lion-Heart. Both had served their cause well, neither had won.

Which do you think was the greater leader?

Activity

To the teacher:

Out of the class select three groups of four or five verbal students for a role-playing activity.

Group A—This group should be all boys, preferably those active in sports. They are to play the part of the school basketball team. They have just been asked by the coach to submit a list of qualifications for the new team captain. They should keep in mind the school's size, the school's spirit, and the school's current playing record.

Group B—This group should be all girls. They are to play the part of the school cheerleaders (pep squad) in the selecting of a new team captain. The girls should make a list of the characteristics they feel an ideal pep squad captain should have.

Group C—This group should be composed of both boys and girls. They are playing the part of the Senior Class Nominating Committee, attempting to select a senior class president. They should discuss and list the qualities they feel are necessary in view of accomplishing the senior class activities, such as the school senior project, the senior prom, Homecoming, senior picnic, etc.

After the role-playing activity, all three lists should be put on the board.

Questions for discussion:

1. What qualifications are about the same on all three lists? Why are they similar?

2. Do you think the present school leaders display these qualities?

3. Does the principal have these qualities? How about the President of the U.S.?

4. List the following in order from the poorest leader to the best leader. Consider ONLY their leadership: Martin Luther King, Winston Churchill, George Washington, Robert E. Lee, Mao Tse-tung, Hitler, Napoleon, our current President, Mohammed.

5. Who do you think is the greatest leader who ever lived?

"THERE AIN'T NO FREE LUNCH"

The comedian Mort Freidberg said, "There ain't no free lunch." What he meant by this was, you can't get something for nothing.

Many people today receive in the mail a notice which says, "You have already won a big prize of $10,000, or a free TV set, or a new wristwatch. All you have to do is fill out the card and perhaps buy the product advertised and send it back and you will receive your prize."

Studies made by the Federal Trade Commission show that most of these claims are fraudulent. That is, there is no free prize and this is just an advertising gimmick to try to get you to buy the product which is promoted by the group which is offering the so-called "free prizes."

All of us seem to have within us a tendency to try to get something for nothing. Why should we not work for the things that we want? After all, many people enjoy working. It gives them a good appetite, it strengthens their bodies, it promotes good health, it brings the joy and satisfaction of having accomplished something.

Many people go to Las Vegas every year in an attempt to get something for nothing. Strangely, if you talk with people who go to Las Vegas, you'll never encounter anyone who has ever lost. People always say, "Well, I just broke even and I had a lot of fun."

Millions and millions of dollars are wasted away in gambling in Las Vegas every year, and that's just the known gambling. The Internal Revenue Service estimates that the unknown, unregulated gambling is more than three times that of the millions and millions of dollars which are taken in at Las Vegas and the other gambling casinos in Nevada every year.

The smart gambler knows you can't get something for nothing. He knows the big hotels in the gambling centers were not built by money that was given away, but instead money that was lost by people who thought they could get something for nothing.

Whenever anyone offers you something for nothing, make very sure that you investigate it very closely because "there ain't no free lunch." You will find in this world very few things that don't have some strings attached. Beware of those which apparently have none.

Activity

To the teacher:

Make a ditto sheet of the following, and put one on each student's desk, facedown. Tell them that when you give the signal, they are to turn the paper over and begin working on it. The first five to finish within the time limit will win a prize (get extra credit, etc.).

Give them the signal to start. Walk around the room to see if anyone has actually done only No. 2 question as stated. This can be easily done within two minutes—the time limit required to read the entire page. Wait until everyone is finished before awarding prizes or announcing extra credit, if any!

This is a timed test!
Can you follow directions?
Can you finish in time?

1. Read everything carefully before you do anything.

2. Put your name in the upper right-hand corner of this paper.

3. Underline the word *time* in the title at the top.

4. Punch three small holes in the upper left-hand corner with your pencil.

5. Put a circle around each hole.

6. Put a square around each circle.

7. Circle the word *time* in sentence No. 3.

8. Write the word *yes* three times after the word *time* in the title.

9. Draw a circle around sentence No. 5.

10. Put an *X* beside the even numbered sentences from 1 to 10 only.

11. Put a check beside the odd numbered sentences from 1 to 10 only.

12. On the back of this paper write your address, including zip code.

13. Underline your last name at the top of the paper.

14. Loudly call out your first name when you get this far.

15. On the reverse side of this paper add the numbers 1980 and 1981.

16. Wad up a piece of paper and put it into the wastebasket.

17. Loudly call out "I am fast and smart!" when you get this far.

18. Put a circle around your answer to sentence No. 15.

19. Now that you have finished reading everything carefully, do only sentence No. 2.

20. Carefully turn your paper over and smile at the teacher.

THE WORLD'S WORST THIEF

(Adapted from the Giant Killer)

Today we are going to talk about the world's worst thief. He steals from the rich and the poor, the famous and the unknown, the old and the young. He steals from those in palaces and even from those in prisons. Worst of all, he acts like your friend but, when you least expect it, he'll strip you without a blink of remorse.

He is master of phoney logic, a quick talker who will rearrange the facts just enough to make them sound plausible, even to you. Often, when caught red-handed by your friends, you will find yourself actually quoting him and defending him. By the time you realize you are his victim, it will be too late. In fact, many never realize how they have lost the very best things in life to this thief. They go through life hand in hand with the very robber who has stripped them of all that is worthwhile.

The chances are that you have met this thief already; if you haven't, it's time you learned his name. PROCRASTINATION! He steals incentive and its partner, motivation. He carries off these priceless valuables and leaves you with excuses, empty promises, phoney reasons, embarrassment, and guilt. He knows the best time to hit you—when you least expect it. For example, it's time to do your homework. You've had a long day and you're tired. You look at the assignment and suddenly the thief is bargaining with you, changing the facts, stealing your will to accomplish, whispering that magic word over and over, "tomorrow, tomorrow," even when you know the next day is too late. By the time you've come to grips with the truth, he is gone and so is your opportunity to get it done.

He's too smart a crook to give you a direct bold-faced lie like, "Homework is unnecessary"; instead, he just slips you a subtle suggestion like, "There's no hurry." He has one basic goal and that's to take everything you ever want or would like to accomplish and leave you with his reward, defeat!

Have you ever met this thief? Would you like to get rid of him?

The way to do so is so simple that you won't believe it. Really. All it takes is just one simple word. If you use this little word at the right time, it carries the wallop of a winner because winners have discovered that the thief can't stand the sound of it. Better still, if you use it often enough, he might find it so distasteful that he may leave you and never come back.

Would you like to know what the word is? OK, I'll make a bargain with you. If you promise to use it the next time the time-stealer comes your way, I'll pass it on to you. But it's like writing a check; it's easy to write, but you have to have money in the bank to back it up!

Likewise, this word is easy to say, but you have to have willpower to back it up and MEAN IT!

Are you ready?

The word is *no*!

Activity

To the teacher:

1. Tell your students they are going to make three wishes. Have them write down three things they would like very much to do.

   a. I would like to learn to be better at sports, surfing, skateboarding, playing a musical instrument, or art.

   b. I would like to visit some special places, such as Disneyland, Hollywood, the mountains, etc.

   c. I would like to make some personal improvements, such as have more money, have more friends, learn to scuba dive, play the uke, get better grades.

2. Next have them rank their wishes as first, second, or third.

3. Now they should consider their first wish and answer the following questions:

   a. What will I need in order to accomplish my wish:

      1. Money?

      2. Equipment?

      3. Instruction?

      4. Special permission?

   b. Is there someone who can help me accomplish my wish? How do I contact this person?

   c. Write at least three steps I must take in order to accomplish my wish.

   d. Write down a realistic schedule or timetable to get my wish accomplished.

4. Each student should do this for all three wishes, then select one of the three he wishes to attempt. The teacher should keep a record of this and discuss the students' progress toward their goals later on in the year.

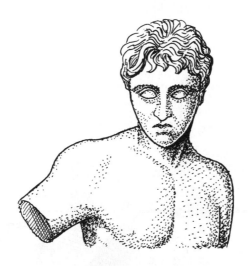

THE LEGEND OF PHLEGNON AND HERODION
(Ancient Greek legend)

The city of Athens was astir. Everyone was discussing the great race to be held tomorrow. Visitors had come from many miles to watch the event, and much money was being wagered on the winner. The heavy betting was on Phlegnon, the famous runner whom everyone loved for his generous, humble manner. Yet there were many who felt Herodion might well win. He almost beat Phlegnon in the last race, but he had lost favor with the crowd because he had left the track cursing Phlegnon, the winner.

Everyone was disappointed when the terrible news reached them, everyone but Herodion, that is. Phlegnon had fallen ill and would be unable to race. The next day Herodion easily crossed the finish line well ahead of the pack. All the citizens applauded politely for him, but they did not cheer wildly as they always had done for Phlegnon. Inside, Herodion burned with envy and rage. He had always been second to Phlegnon and he was still so, even in victory.

Horror and grief filled the city when the physicians announced the death of Phlegnon. "A statue must be erected to honor him," said everyone as the city mourned its beloved hero. A magnificent sparkling white figure was eventually raised in the central square. No one noticed Herodion standing in the crowd.

"This was surely a great athlete. His statue looks almost as though it's about to move."

"Herodion is a pretty good runner, too."

"Oh yes, he's good, but he'll never be as great as Phlegnon."

The two citizens moved away leaving Herodion glaring in envious hatred up at the face of the man who had always beaten him and who, even in death, was his better.

When darkness fell, all the crowd left but one, Herodion. From his hiding place, he brought out his sharp chisel and heavy hammer and began to chip away great chunks of marble. Finally, only one piece remained holding the grand figure erect. With one last mighty heave of the hammer, the supporting marble fell away. The great statue wobbled slightly, and then came crashing down on top of Herodion, killing him instantly with crushing force.

Herodion had been killed by his own envy and jealousy; but before we feel smug about Herodion, remember that it is a disease from which we all may suffer. Jealousy will destroy a wonderful friendship; it will instantly dissolve a budding romance. It will destroy the productive work of a group of professionals; it will cause a well-drilled team to fall apart, all because it will question honest motives and deplore another's success. It makes once warm comrades turn severe, suspicious, narrow and negative.

Here is the tortured cry of Shakespeare's Othello when he fears he is losing his beloved Desdemona:

> I had rather be a toad
> And live upon the vapor of a dungeon
> Than keep a corner in the thing I love
> For other users. (*Othello* Act III, Sc. iii)

Don't you be a toad in a dungeon of your own making; live in glorious sunlight or open appreciation of those who out-perform you.

Activity

To the teacher:

Ask your students to fold a sheet of paper into four columns. In the first column, write a list of five people whom they come in daily contact with. They might include their teachers, friends, parents, brothers or sisters, classmates or teammates, if they play some sort of sports.

In the second column, they should write opposite at least three of the people, "The thing that bothers me about this person is . . . ." Example: "The thing that bothers me about Jim is that he never helps to do his share of the work." Or, "The thing that bothers me about Jane is that she always wants to be the captain."

After your students have written at least three statements about what bothers them concerning these people they have listed, tell them they are now going to write down what they would like to have changed in the individual. Example: "The thing that bothers me about Jim is that he never helps with his share of the work, and I want him to pitch in and help get the work done from now on." Or: "The thing that bothers me about Jane is that she always wants to be the team captain, and I want her to just be one of the team."

In the fourth column, write down something about the individual that you appreciate. Example:

1. The thing that bothers me about Jim is that he never helps with his share of the work,

   and I want him to pitch in and help get the work done from now on,

   but I appreciate the fact that he plays several sports and doesn't have much time left.

2. The thing that bothers me about Jane is that she always wants to be the team captain,

   and I want her to just be one of the team,

   but I appreciate the fact that she plays most sports very well.

Don't be fearful of permitting your students to write down things that bother them about their fellow classmates or family and friends. It's probably that these things are there anyway, and it's best to let them be discussed in a positive manner, rather than let them be suppressed.

HANS, THE TRUSTWORTHY

(A true story of old Germany)

"That poor ragged Hans. I feel so sorry for him. He'll never amount to anything now that his parents are gone."

Two of the village women were washing their clothes near the central fountain.

"Why, I thought Herr Huber had engaged him to care for his flock of sheep."

"Oh, yes, but he pays him little or nothing. Just a place to sleep and a little food. It's a public disgrace."

Hans could not hear this conversation, partly because of the fountain, but mostly because of the bleating of the sheep as he moved them through the village up onto the mountain. Far away through the clouds, the jagged snow peaks thrust their spires into the skies, but between them and the village lay the great green forest. Hans knew about where he wanted to take the flock, but there were few paths, and he must rely upon his own inner sense of direction through the tangle of trees and undergrowth. About midday, he reached his objective—a small patch of sweet, green grass, a carpet of tender nutrient for his flock.

Hans had been there but a moment when a horse broke through the trees and a tall man in hunter's clothing rode up to him.

"Hey there, lad, which way to the nearest village? I'm afraid I'm a bit lost."

"It's that way, sir," said Hans. "But I'm afraid you'll never find it. There are no paths, just a few sheep tracks."

"I must reach the village before sundown. I'll pay you well; three pieces of silver, if you'll show me the way."

Hans thought of the silver. It would be enough to buy himself a new pair of shoes for the coming winter. But then he shook his head. "No, I cannot leave the sheep. They will stray into the woods to be devoured by the wolves."

"No matter, my boy. I will pay you five pieces of silver. That is enough to buy several sheep, and I'll give you five more when we reach the village."

"Sir, I cannot go. These are my master's sheep, and I am responsible for them. If they are lost I will not have kept my word to care for them."

"I understand. Suppose I stay with your sheep while you go and fetch a guide for me?"

"No, you have already tried to get me to break my word to my master. How can I trust you to keep your word to me?"

The hunter laughed, "You are a stubborn one. I wish I could trust my servants as much as your master can trust you."

Just then several men rode out of the woods.

"Oh there you are, Your Majesty. We have been searching everywhere for you."

Hans trembled when he learned that the hunter was none other than the Royal Prince Rupert, himself. He need not have feared, for the Prince came over to him and, putting his hand on his shoulder, said, "You are a fine, trustworthy boy. What is your name?"

"Hans, Sir."

"Hans, what?"

"I do not have a surname, Sir. My parents are dead and my master does not wish me to use his name."

"We shall see about that," the Prince replied, and rode off into the woods with the others following.

A few days later, the women were washing again at the fountain.

"Have you heard? The Prince himself is coming to the village today!"

The mayor and all the village officials were on hand to greet him, but the Prince did not stop at the City Hall. Instead, he rode right on down to the end of the street to the sheep pens. To the villager's amazement, he knocked on the door of Hans' little shepherd's hut. Hans bowed low when he saw who had come.

"Hans, I want you to come with me. I know you are a young man whom I can trust."

"I will come if my master can find another to take my place with the sheep."

The Prince turned to his steward in sharp command. "Take care of that! See his master!"

As the Prince and Hans rode off together, one of the washer women turned to the other and said, "A mighty fine boy. A real credit to his community. I always knew he would do well."

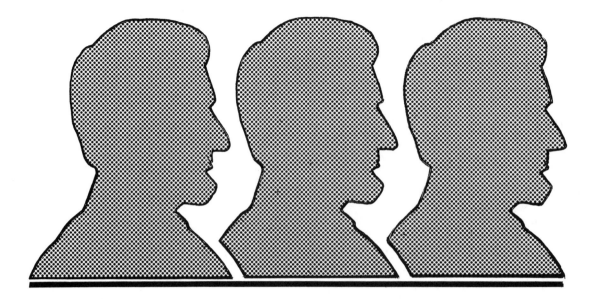

Activity

To the teacher:

Tell your class that they are going to play the famous television game *To Tell the Truth.* Select three students to be volunteer contestants. Give each one of them a 3″ x 5″ card with the following information on it:

No. 1:

My name is Abraham Lincoln. I was born on March 12, 1809, in Kentucky and served as fourteenth President of the United States, during which time it was my duty to attempt to preserve the Union. After one of the battles of the Civil War, I was called upon to give a speech at Atlanta, Georgia, in which I said, ". . . government of the people, by the people, and for the people shall not perish from the earth." On the night of April 14, 1865, while attending a theatre, I was attacked and shot by John Wilkes Booth.

No. 2:

My name is Abraham Lincoln. I served as sixteenth President of the United States. I rose to that high position from a log cabin where I taught myself to read and write using candlelight at night after a hard day's work. It was my duty as President to put down the Southern rebellion known as the Civil War. I gave many speeches during my presidency. In one of them I said, "You can fool some of the people all of the time, and all of the people some of the time, but you can't fool all of the people all of the time."

No. 3:

My name is Abraham Lincoln. I served as President of the United States from 1861 to 1865. During that period, America was divided by a great Civil War in which almost every family in both North and South suffered some loss. I was born on February 12, 1809, and lived most of my life in Illinois before I became President. I was happily married and I had four sons, one of whom (Tad Lincoln) served in the Union Army with some distinction. On April 6, 1865, after the war was over, I said, "I would prefer only the intelligent Blacks and those who gave service in the Union Army to be given the right to vote."

Have the volunteer contestants come up and sit in front of the class. Give each of them a card to read. After they have read their statements, the class may ask any one of them to re-read any part or all of their statements over again as many times as they wish.

After all the questioning is finished, the class is asked to vote on the REAL Abraham Lincoln, either No. 1, No. 2, or No. 3. Once the class has decided, then the teacher should ask the REAL Abraham Lincoln to stand up. (In this case, No. 2, the one with a star on his card.)

The example given here is Abraham Lincoln; however the teacher could make up cards for any well-known person, depending upon the interests of the class.

FLIGHT INTO NOTHING

(The Bermuda Triangle)

"Calling tower, this is an emergency . . . we seem to be off course . . . we cannot see land . . . repeat . . . we cannot see land . . . ."

The speaker of this message was Lieutenant Charles C. Taylor, U.S. Navy, leader of five torpedo bombers of Flight 19 from the Florida coastline to Chicken Shoals in the Bahamas, on December 5, 1945.

The control tower at Fort Lauderdale Navel Air Station, Florida, quickly responded, "What is your position?"

"We're not sure of our position. We can't be sure just where we are. We seem to be lost." This was an astounding reply for an experienced flight leader to make, but the tower replied in a calm steady manner.

"Assume bearing due West."

Lieutenant Taylor's reply had a mysterious quality that has been studied by experts ever since. "We don't know which way is West. Everything is wrong . . . strange . . . we can't be sure of any direction. Even the ocean doesn't look as it should."

Flight 19 did not know it, but they were flying directly into history. Books, films, and even poems have been written about their disappearance. They flew into the oblivion of "The Triangle of Death," "The Hoo Doo Sea," and most recently "The Bermuda Triangle." This is a vast stretch of ocean bounded roughly by Bermuda on the North, Puerto Rico on the South, and Florida on the West.

The disappearance of five airplanes and their flight crews caused widespread concern by the naval authorities, but worse was to follow. A large flying boat was dispatched on a rescue mission to find Flight 19, but once it left Fort Lauderdale, it also flew into radio silence and oblivion, even though the tower attempted to reach it by radio almost immediately after it was airborne.

After a long investigation, one of the officers concluded, "They vanished as completely as if they had flown to Mars!"

In his well-known book entitled, *The Bermuda Triangle,* author Charles Berlitz details the known disappearances of 141 different aircraft of all types—light planes, jets, cargo and passenger planes—within the mystery area between 1945 and 1976. Of this vast number, not one bit of wreckage or debris has ever been found, although many of these crafts were among the largest aircraft ever built. What mysterious force seems to snatch these planes from the sky?

The theorists speculate on such unlikely causes as disintegrated rays emerging from a subterranean power source placed on the seabed by former inhabitants of the earth. Time and space warps are popular among some writers. Others suggest that planes do not come down into the water, but rather they are forced up into outer space by some kind of a reversal of gravity. The sea in that area does have some curious properties discovered by none other than Christopher Columbus himself.

On the night before he was to set foot on the New World, Columbus recorded that he observed a great bolt of fire which shot across the sky and fell into the ocean. As he sailed on, he recorded a mysterious glow from the sea long after sunset. Two modern explorers in the spacecraft *Apollo 12* reported these same luminous streaks were the last visible light they could see as they left the earth.

Not all investigators take such a sensational view. Author Lawrence Kusche of *The Bermuda Triangle Mystery Solved* debunks the whole idea of anything unusual about this area of the earth, saying that it just happens to be one of the busiest sea and air traffic lanes in the world, in his opinion.

Isaac Asimov, science fiction author, writes, "I do not think that anything is essentially unexplainable. There are things that are unexplained. They may never be explained, because we do not have sufficient data available yet to explain them." Man has always attributed magic and exotic causes to those things he does not understand. Eclipses and earthquakes were thought to herald the wrath of the gods, until they could be explained. We apparently need some very special studies to help us better understand this part of the world. Until then we must be careful to distinguish between fact and fiction before we come to any conclusions.

Activity

To the teacher:

Tell your class they are all going to imagine they are part of a team of outer space scientists that have come in a UFO to visit and study our planet Earth.

Put the following list of specialties on the board and split the class into teams of three to five students for each specialty, depending upon the size of your class.

UFO Outer Space Team Specialties

1. Religion and belief system

2. Economics and money systems

3. Food and energy production and consumption

4. Use of the natural environment

5. Law enforcement and governmental systems

Have each team gather in a separate part of the room. Then announce each team will be given the name of a familiar location from which they must write their report. They must imagine various observations of how Earth people do things with regard to their specialties.

The teacher should then give each team (confidentially) the following locations (or any the teacher may choose):

A. To the religion team: A football game

B. To the economics team: McDonald's

C. To the food and energy team: A beer distillery

D. To the law enforcement team: A hospital

E. To the environment team: An airport

After each team has the opportunity to write its imaginary report, they should select one of their members to report their findings to the rest of the teams. The rest of the class must now guess WHERE the reporting team made their observations. The team with the least guesses is the winner.

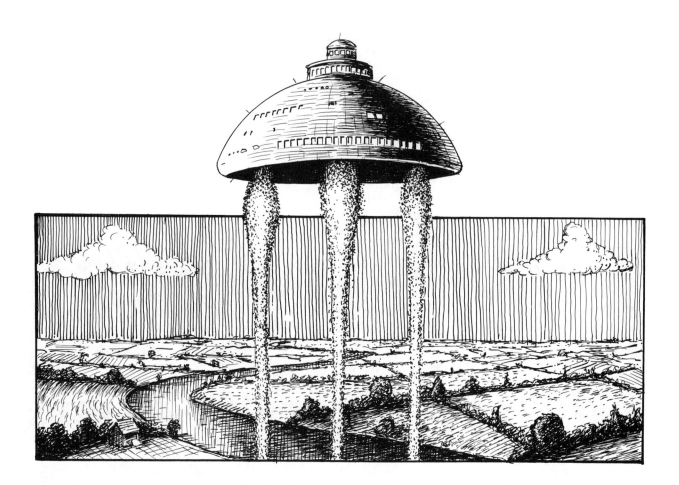

Questions for discussion:

1. How do you think UFO scientists would evaluate the way we treat each other?

2. Do people tend to do something just because everyone else is also doing it?

3. Would UFO scientists have a better or worse view of Earth people if they were to visit Russia?

4. If you were a UFO space scientist, how would you evaluate earth people on the following statements? Mark each one yes, no, or maybe.

    A. Humans tend to regard their actions as logical. _____

    B. Humans tend to conform. _____

    C. Humans tend to yield to repetition of stimuli. _____

    D. Humans tend to believe what they want to believe,
       regardless of the facts. _____

    E. Humans tend to accept ideas from those they like. _____

    F. Humans tend to act immediately when persuaded. _____

I SHOULD HAVE BEEN LISTENING INSTEAD OF TALKING

A wise old owl sat on an oak.
The more he saw, the less he spoke.
The less he spoke, the more he heard.
Now, why can't we all be like that old bird?

We all like to talk, but it seems that no one really wants to listen. Lots of people today need to do more listening.

Recently, a very large corporation hired a man at an enormous salary—simply because he was a good listener. He had sympathy for people who had troubles, worries, and all sorts of things that were bothering them. The employees of this large corporation soon sensed that he was one who would listen and who could be trusted. He wouldn't repeat what he heard, and so they came and confided their troubles and all their worries to him. They found after they had spoken with him, they were better able to go back and do their work when they went back to the job.

Careful listening is also a means by which we learn valuable information. There are lots of people that we should listen to very carefully. Certainly, we should listen to our own parents, regardless of how old they are, because parents want us to do the things that are the best in life. They already have been down the road and know where all the bends and turns and the kinks are. They know where the holes and the bumps are in the road. If we'll but listen to them, then they can steer us around the bad parts of life and keep us headed on the straight and smooth road.

Next, we should listen to our teachers, whether they be in the classroom of the public school or the classroom of the university. They help us to find out what is in our textbooks. They also want to help us discuss our problems. Often, by talking to our teachers, we can resolve a problem simply by having a better opportunity to look at it, examine it, and take it apart to see what all the aspects of the problem are.

Lastly, and most importantly, we should listen to our own conscience—that still, small voice which is inside of us, telling us about right and wrong. If we turn it off too often, if we don't listen, then after a while it stops speaking to us.

Chief Sitting Bull, the famous Indian leader who overcame the Sixth Cavalry at the battle often called Custer's Massacre, said once, "My conscience is like a little wheel that turns inside of me. It hurts, but if I ignore it, after a while the wheel becomes smooth, and I don't feel it any more."

Activity

To the teacher:

1. Have your students choose partners so the whole class is divided into teams of two. If one is left over, that student should team up with the teacher.

2. Explain to your students that they are going to take turns talking to each other to find out how well they can listen. Each person is to talk for three minutes about his parents, telling what he thinks is important about them. After three minutes, they swap; the listener becomes the talker and vice versa.

When a person is talking, he should not be interrupted with questions. When both partners have had their turns, explain that now we are going to find out how well they listened to each other. The listener now tells his partner how he (the partner) feels about his parents. When this is done, the partner then decides whether or not he was accurate. They now reverse, with the other partner going through the same process.

Questions for discussion:

1. Did you prefer to be the talker or the listener? Why?

2. Do you listen to your parents as well as you listened to your partner?

3. Were you surprised when your partner was able (or not able) to determine how you feel toward your parents?

4. How much listening takes place in the school cafeteria?

5. Do people tell you things other than what they say in words, body language, tone, and expression of voice?

Have your students now repeat the process with a new partner and a new topic. Each talker now gives a complete description of himself for three minutes. When both partners have had their turn, they should write down the answer to this question. What did each person feel were the most important qualities about himself?

For dramatic effect, the teacher could single out one student and purposely tell him to ignore his partner while he is talking. Then later, ask the "slighted" partner how he felt when he was not listened to.

THE LEGENDARY JOHNNY APPLESEED

"The Lord is good to me,
And so I thank the Lord
For giving me
The things I need:
The sun and rain . . .
        And the appleseed.
The Lord is good to me!"

The Ballad of Johnny Appleseed

The Western frontier of America was accustomed to travelling preachers, but one of the most colorful of God's servants preached not religion (although he always carried a Bible) but the harmony of nature. Because he distributed apple seeds wherever he went, he was popularly known as Johnny Appleseed, although his real name was John Chapman. No one is sure when or where he was born, but it is probable that he began life in a major eastern city about the time of the American independence.

As a young lad, he often would be gone for several weeks at a time, roaming and exploring the primitive wilderness which was so readily accessible in those days. During that period, he came to know and love all plants and make friends with all animals. One story tells of how he even became friendly with a snake that bit him.

Not only did he carefully plant apples wherever he went, but he also was widely recognized as an expert on plant and tree diseases. When a pioneer farmer was having trouble with his crop or fruit orchard, he would send for Johnny Appleseed. It would sometimes require him to stay on the farm for an entire season to discover the problem and recommend a cure. Not only did he help sick plants but also sick people. Johnny always carried with him a bag of medicinal herbs for two reasons: to minister to the sick and to plant these medicinal herbs in new places for those living on the frontier. There is little doubt these plants were of immense value when physicians were few and far between.

Johnny's love for nature and his friendly, unassuming ways won him great respect from the Indians, who considered him one of their own people.

As the white man cut down the forest and killed the animals, the Indians became more and more incensed, until finally war was inevitable. A great host of Indian warriors gathered to destroy the white settlement and burn the farms. A white man's council was called, and it was decided that only Johnny Appleseed could possibly get through to bring soldiers to protect them.

"You had better leave at midnight, so you won't be noticed," it was suggested.

"I will be noticed no matter when I go. No, I will leave at noon tomorrow."

So Johnny rode out on his old mare the next day. The chief of the Indians met him after he had gone a short distance.

"Where you go, Appleman?"

"I go to bring soldiers and cannon. You must leave this place now, or there will be much blood and dying." With that, Johnny rode off to get help and warn other settlers. When the troops arrived, the Indians were gone. Johnny had saved the lives of both the red and white men, since they both had believed in him.

When he was an old man, Johnny was called to a faraway state to help a farmer save his orchard. During the trip, he caught pneumonia and died, still trying to help others. The whole nation was saddened to hear of his death. He was never rich, he wore tattered old clothes and was often hungry. He had no political power or social influence, but he won the love and respect of all those who knew him, and many of the trees and herbs he planted are alive and flourishing today, just as his memory is alive in the hearts of many Americans.

Activity

To the teacher:

Here is a chance to talk about the idea of large numbers, which most children love.

Make a ditto sheet or put on the board the following table:

Million = 1,000,000 (6 zeros or 10^6)

Billion = 1,000,000,000 (9 zeros or 10^9)

Trillion = 1,000,000,000,000 (12 zeros or 10^{12})

(There is no such thing as a zillion.)

Quadrillion = 1,000,000,000,000,000 (15 zeros or 10^{15})

Quintillion = 1,000,000,000,000,000,000 (18 zeros or 10^{18})

Sextillion = 1,000,000,000,000,000,000,000 (21 zeros or 10^{21})

Septillion = 1,000,000,000,000,000,000,000,000 (24 zeros or 10^{24})

Octillion = 1,000,000,000,000,000,000,000,000,000 (27 zeros or 10^{27})

Nonillion = 1,000,000,000,000,000,000,000,000,000,000 (30 zeros)

Decillion = 1,000,000,000,000,000,000,000,000,000,000,000 (33 zeros)

A Googal = 1 followed by 100 zeros. The largest named number.

Some interesting questions:

1. What does a million really mean? (A thousand thousands)

2. How long ago was a million days? (Eighth century, B.C.)

3. How far is a million inches? (About 16 miles)

4. How long from now is a billion seconds? (Beginning of the twenty-first century)

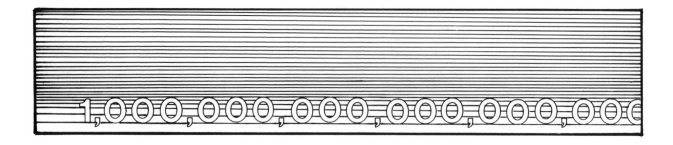

5. Which of these numbers is the biggest?

   100^4 $1,000^3$ $10,000^2$ $(1,000^3)$

6. The Greeks did a lot of things in mathematics. Their name for 10,000 was a "myriad." Can you write Archimedes' "myriad or myriads" as a number? (10,000 × 10,000 = 1,000,000,000)

7. Why do you suppose Archimedes called this number an octade? (Because it has 8 places)

8. The Dutch merchant, Peter Minuit, paid the Indians of New York only $24 for the island of Manhattan in 1626. If we covered Manhattan today completely with dollar bills, it would take more than 5 followed by 9 zeros, and this would still not pay for the island. Can you name this amount in words? (5,000,000,000 = 5 billion)

9. The center of our Milky Way Galaxy is about 30,000 "light years" away from our solar system. If a "light year" is 6 followed by 12 zeros in miles, how far away are we from the center of our galaxy? (18 followed by 16 zeros miles)

10. Our Milky Way Galaxy is thought to contain more than 100,000,000,000 stars like our sun. What is this number in words? (one hundred billion)

CONFUCIUS THE WISE

(Adapted from the Hsiao King)

Perhaps you have heard of the wise counselor Confucius, who lived many centuries ago in China. He gave advice to all who came to him with difficult problems. In China, children are taught at an early age to respect and obey their parents and grandparents. Older people are highly respected.

One day a young man came to Confucius with a very difficult question. He said, "Master, I know I should listen to my parents and be obedient to their wishes to avoid troubles in my life, but I would like to ask you; should I obey every command of my parents? What if they tell me to do something I know to be wrong?"

"Ah," said Confucius. "Let me tell you the story of a great king who lived long ago in a far off kingdom. Because he was very rich and powerful, he thought he could do anything he wished. So he began to break the promises he had made through treaties with the neighboring kingdoms. He raised taxes and jailed many of his people. Fortunately, he had seven wise ministers who were brave enough to come to him and warn him that if he continued to do wrong things he would lose his kingdom. He thought a long time about what they had said, and then he decided to heed their advice and, as a result, he kept his throne."

"Then there was a prince whose father gave him a great castle with rich lands surrounding it. But he was as lazy as a crocodile lying in the sun. He began to spend his money, throwing it around like a farmer's wife feeding her chickens. He would have lost it all, except one day five of his friends came to him to tell him that he must stop before he lost everything. He was angry at first, but then he changed his ways and saved his castle and lands."

"Finally, there was once a governor of a great land who ruled his country wisely and well, but unknown to anyone else, he had very bad habits of alcohol and gambling. Three of his officers came to him and told him that soon everyone would know of his bad habits and that unless he changed, he would be quickly out of office. Although it was very hard at first, the governor forced himself to give up his bad habits, and he was able to serve his country for many years."

"Now, each of these rulers had a difficult lesson to learn from those who were under their orders. In the same way, a father or leader must listen and change his ways when he is doing something wrong. It is the right, indeed, it is the duty of each one of us to say 'no' when we are told to do something wrong. The child must say to his parent, 'I cannot permit you to bring shame upon yourself and upon me by obeying your command to do what is wrong.' "

Confucius thus gave to the Chinese people a rule to follow. When you are told to do something wrong, you must not do it, out of respect to yourself and to those who might suffer by your wrongdoing.

(In our modern day, many young men had to decide whether they should go to Vietnam to fight and kill the Vietnamese people even though they were ordered by their government to do so.)

Activity

To the teacher:

Have your students take three pieces of paper from their notebooks. On the first sheet of paper, they should write:

(1) The person I would most desire to be like is _____ .
    This individual may be historical (Joan of Arc), imaginary (Superman), or living now (Muhammad Ali).

They are then to write down at least five worthwhile characteristics of this person.

On the second sheet of paper, students should write:

(2) The person I do **not** wish to be like is _____ .
    Again they should list the personality traits which they feel are undesirable.

On the third sheet of paper, they should write:

(3) If I wish to be a leader, what traits should I acquire? (Write a list.) What traits should I avoid?

Students might now share their selections and reasons with the rest of the class. The teacher should list common characteristics on the chalkboard. An interesting closing exercise is to select two verbal students, one representing a positive figure (Abraham Lincoln) and one representing a negative figure (Darth Vader) from those suggested by the class. Then have them give an imaginary debate over one of the following topics:

1. Which is true? Government exists to serve the people, or people exist to serve the government?

2. The common good of all is more important than the individual good of one person.

3. It is all right to tell untruths to people as long as it is for their own good.

BIBLIOGRAPHY

Aiken, H.D., *The Age of Ideology: The 19th Century Philosophers*, New York: Mentor Books, 1956.

Burke, John, *An Illustrated History of England*, Oxford: Blackwell, 1980.

Chomsky, N., *Language and the Mind*, New York: Harcourt, Brace and World, 1968.

Dalis, Gus T. et al., *Values Education*, Los Angeles: Office of the Los Angeles County Superintendent, 1974.

Dewey, John, *Human Nature and Conduct*, New York: Modern Library, 1950.

Fowler, J., and Sam Keen, *Life Maps*, Chicago: Zondervan, 1980.

Fraenkel, Jack R., *Helping Students Think and Value*, Englewood Cliffs, N.J.: Prentice-Hall, Inc., 1973.

——————— . *How to Teach About Values*, Englewood Cliffs, N.J.: Prentice-Hall, Inc., 1976.

Galbraith, Ronald et al., *Moral Reasoning*, Amoka, Minn.: Greenhaven Press, 1976.

Goldman, Alvin, *A Theory of Human Action*, Englewood Cliffs, N.J.: Prentice-Hall, Inc., 1969.

Kohlberg, Lawrence, *"Moral Stages & Moralization,"* The Cognitive Development Approach, *Man, Morality, and Society*, Edited by Thomas Lickona. New York: Holt, Rinehart and Winston, 1971.

Mandelbrot, Benoit, *Fractals: Form, Chance & Dimension*, San Francisco: W.H. Freeman & Co., 1977.

Medawar, Sir Peter, "On 'The Effecting of All Things Possible,'" The Advancement of Science 26, 1-9 (1969-1970).

Morison, Robert S., *Towards a Common Scale of Measurement*, New York: Daedalus, Vol. 94, No. 1, 1965.

National Education Association, *Value Concepts and Techniques*, Washington, D.C.: National Education Association of the United States, 1976.

Piaget, Jean, *The Moral Judgement of the Child*, Glencoe, Ill.: Free Press, 1948.

Raths, Louis E. et al., *Values Teaching*, Columbus, Ohio: Charles Merrill Publishing Co., 1966.

Schoeck, Helmut, and James W. Wiggins, *Scientism and Values*, Princeton, N.J.: Van Nostrand, 1960.

Simon, Howe, and Kirschenbaum, *Values Clarification, a Handbook of Practical Strategies for Teachers and Students*, New York: Hart Publishing, 1972.

Stent, Gunther S., *Paradoxes in Progress,* San Francisco: W.H. Freeman, 1978.

Von Wright, G.H., *Explanation and Understanding*, Ithica, N.Y.: Cornell University, 1971.